Making Divorce Work

"*Making Divorce Work* is an absolutely essential work. This is the book everyone getting divorced needs to get through the difficulties of breaking up and going on with your life. Divorce clears the way for a new beginning, but it is too often a bad beginning unless people make use of the wise and practical advice this book contains. And this book is especially a must-read for people with children. I am thrilled to be able to recommend this book to people who need it."

—Mira Kirshenbaum,
author of *Too Good to Leave, Too Bad to Stay*
and *When Good People Have Affairs*

"*Making Divorce Work* translates Diana and Katie's unique mediation model into skills anyone can use and that will revolutionize the way people get divorced."
—Len Jacoby,
founder of Jacoby & Meyers Law Offices

"Imagine a world in which instead of ruining your life, your divorce could help you redefine your goals for yourself and your family. Now there is a book that shows you how to make this happen in eight simple steps: *Making Divorce Work*."
—Nell Merlino, author of *Stepping Out of Line*,
CEO and founder of Count Me In for Women's Economic Independence,
and the creative force behind Take Our Daughters to Work Day

"I am going to give a copy of *Making Divorce Work* to any friend or family member who is confronted with this situation. And I am most grateful to Mercer and Wennechuk for showing me how to make my own marriage stronger and more fulfilling."

—Wiliam D. Henderson,
professor at Indiana University Maurer School of Law

continued . . .

"One of the saddest episodes we can go through in life is to engage in pitched battle with someone to whom we once said adoringly, 'I do.' Divorce is agonizing enough for many of us, without the added heartbreak of venom and hatred spewing into the lives of family and friends—especially children, whose stability is being ripped apart and whose loyalty may be torn between Mom and Dad. Here now comes a book that is chock-full of simple, everyday, practical steps that can ease our way through a minefield so we come out not just with our sanity intact, but actually far more conscious as individuals. Its countless insights show how a breakup—whether we want it or wish to God it weren't happening—can end up actually advancing our well-being. You'll use *Making Divorce Work* as a daily manual, shoring up every facet of your life from emotional to financial. Save yourself a lot of pain—and share it with friends who are already in pain." —David Robert Ord, author of *Your Forgotten Self* and *Lessons in Loving*

"Many divorce books can be read; this book must be studied. The authors not only intuitively and insightfully understand what people going through divorce need and how they feel, they also offer self-help tools such as writing a divorce mission statement to help readers prepare for success through this life-challenging event. I predict that in the future people will select their professionals, in part, as to whether this book is front and center in their client libraries and whether the divorce professional can use *Making Divorce Work* as a client guide to supplement their competent advice and expertise." —Forrest (Woody) Mosten, collaborative lawyer, mediator, and author of *Collaborative Divorce Handbook* and *The Complete Guide to Mediation*

"Mercer and Wennechuk have written a wise and thoughtful book that will spare anyone going through a divorce much trauma. This is how law ought to be practiced—with compassion for the lives of those going through a major life change, and pragmatic and grounded advice for making life on the other side not only possible but powerful." —Lauren Robel, Dean and Val Nolan Professor at Indiana University Maurer School of Law

"It is said that the emotional impact of divorce is up there with traumas such as a death of a loved one and moving house. It is also likely there are only a few other human experiences guaranteed to bring out the worst in us. There are many who today live with ongoing regret and shame for their unconscious reactive behavior because of a disastrous divorce experience—not to mention the number of children emotionally scarred because of it. This gloomy scenario is no longer necessary. *Making Divorce Work* brings consciousness, clarity, practical applicable wisdom, and common sense insight into what is undeniably one of the most heart-wrenching experiences any human being may have to face. Mercer and Wennechuk skillfully provide us with a practical, conscious, creative, and healing tool to support not only those moving through this experience but also those wishing to be of greater support when their loved ones are faced with such an extreme life change. Divorce no longer has to be the emotional tsunami we have been programmed to anticipate—now it can serve as an opportunity for experiencing profound growth in personal relationships, emotional development, and as a platform from which to creatively initiate a transformed life experience."

—Michael Brown,
author of *The Presence Process* and *Alchemy of the Heart*

"When I studied law nearly fifty years ago, divorces were granted on the basis of 'fault.' Today fault is no longer a legal issue, but cultural influences still bring fault into the dissolution process, which is too often filled with disappointment, anger, and grief. This book walks the reader through the various provocations and events that can take place in the dissolution process and provides common-sense, helpful suggestions on how to envision and pursue a successful life during and after the dissolution. The purpose of this book is not to reduce the divorce rate, which has been steady at 40 percent, but to reduce the negativity and recovery time associated with it."

—Gerald L. Bepko, chancellor emeritus
at Indiana University–Purdue University Indianapolis,
and former dean at IU School of Law Indianapolis

continued . . .

"*Making Divorce Work* is a fresh approach to a topic that has received much attention but continues to be a significant transition and painful process with long-term implications for the health of all family members. With all of the self-help books that have been written about divorce, what possibly could be new to say? These authors offer practical and down-to-earth advice for managing difficult feelings and cultivating the co-parenting relationship so that you can live with yourself—and your ex—during and after the divorce. The authors' emphasis on finding inner peace, and turning that peace outwards gives the message that you can divorce in a way that facilitates learning about yourself, taking responsibility for your actions, dealing peaceably with your ex, and liking who you are even better at the end of the day. This is no easy feat to accomplish, but *Making Divorce Work* will make you feel like it is truly an attainable goal."

—Marsha Kline Pruett, PhD, MSL,
coauthor of *Your Divorce Advisor*

"Read this book before you talk to a lawyer! You will save yourself tons of heartache, talk, and money. If you already have a lawyer, read this before you utter another word to them. Share this book with a friend or family member who is divorcing; it will be the kindest, most generous thing you could ever do for them. They will thank you and their children will thank you—for years to come. This book is a game changer!"

—Lisa Earle McLeod,
author of *The Triangle of Truth* and *Forget Perfect*

"This book provides focused insights, useful strategies, and wise counsel—from the perspective of mediators who have witnessed the dangers of ignoring the truth of their advice. Buy it and keep it by your bedside throughout your dissolution process!"

—Frederick Hertz, lawyer/mediator,
author of *Making It Legal*

MAKING
DIVORCE
WORK

8 Essential Keys to Resolving Conflict
and Rebuilding Your Life

DIANA MERCER, JD
and KATIE JANE WENNECHUK, MA

A PERIGEE BOOK

A PERIGEE BOOK
Published by the Penguin Group
Penguin Group (USA) Inc.
375 Hudson Street, New York, New York 10014, USA
Penguin Group (Canada), 90 Eglinton Avenue East, Suite 700, Toronto, Ontario M4P 2Y3, Canada
(a division of Pearson Penguin Canada Inc.)
Penguin Books Ltd., 80 Strand, London WC2R 0RL, England
Penguin Group Ireland, 25 St. Stephen's Green, Dublin 2, Ireland (a division of Penguin Books Ltd.)
Penguin Group (Australia), 250 Camberwell Road, Camberwell, Victoria 3124, Australia
(a division of Pearson Australia Group Pty. Ltd.)
Penguin Books India Pvt. Ltd., 11 Community Centre, Panchsheel Park, New Delhi—110 017, India
Penguin Group (NZ), 67 Apollo Drive, Rosedale, North Shore 0632, New Zealand
(a division of Pearson New Zealand Ltd.)
Penguin Books (South Africa) (Pty.) Ltd., 24 Sturdee Avenue, Rosebank, Johannesburg 2196,
South Africa
Penguin Books Ltd., Registered Offices: 80 Strand, London WC2R 0RL, England

While the author has made every effort to provide accurate telephone numbers and Internet addresses at the time of publication, neither the publisher nor the author assumes any responsibility for errors or for changes that occur after publication. Further, the publisher does not have any control over and does not assume any responsibility for author or third-party websites or their content.

Copyright © 2010 by Diana Mercer, JD, and Katie Jane Wennechuk, MA
Text design by Kristin del Rosario

First edition: December 2010

Library of Congress Cataloging-in-Publication Data

Mercer, Diana, 1964–
    Making divorce work : 8 essential keys to resolving conflict and rebuilding your life / Diana Mercer and Katie Jane Wennechuk.—1st ed.
        p.   cm.
    Includes index.
    ISBN 978-0-399-53623-6
    1. Divorce.   2. Divorced people—Psychology.   3. Conflict management.   I. Wennechuk, Katie Jane.   II. Title.
    HQ814.M43 2010
    306.89—dc22   2010029630

PRINTED IN THE UNITED STATES OF AMERICA

10 9 8 7 6 5 4 3 2 1

PUBLISHER'S NOTE: This publication is designed to provide accurate and authoritative information in regard to the subject matter covered. It is sold with the understanding that the publisher is not engaged in rendering legal, accounting, or other professional services. If you require legal advice or other expert assistance, you should seek the services of a competent professional. All names and identifying characteristics have been changed to protect the privacy of the individuals involved.

Most Perigee books are available at special quantity discounts for bulk purchases for sales promotions, premiums, fund-raising, or educational use. Special books, or book excerpts, can also be created to fit specific needs. For details, write: Special Markets, Penguin Group (USA) Inc., 375 Hudson Street, New York, New York 10014.

This book is dedicated to all of the courageous couples
who mediate at Peace Talks and
in mediators' offices all over the world.
You teach us something new every day.

CONTENTS

GETTING THE MOST FROM
MAKING DIVORCE WORK

We suggest that you get a notebook to write in while you are reading this book. We'll prompt you in each chapter to express your thoughts on the exercises contained in that chapter. The simple act of writing in your notebook is a very easy way to make changes in your life and set a new direction in motion.

CHAPTER 1

A Divorce That Works

You can create peace on earth, one family at a time.
—DIANA MERCER AND KATIE JANE WENNECHUK

What This Book Will Do for You

This book will change the way you think about divorce. You can get divorced without ruining your life. We know that sounds improbable, if not impossible, but we can show you how to dissolve your marriage and move on without losing your shirt or your sanity—and emerge a better person. And although our examples feature married, heterosexual couples, our advice applies equally to domestic partnerships, same-sex couples, and never married parents.

The divorce rate among recent first marriages is 67 percent. That is two out of three couples! So isn't it about time we stopped scorching the earth using lawyers and courts as weapons and found a better way to say good-bye?

Rather than see it as something that will destroy your family, your divorce can be a way to redefine and rebuild your family and improve your quality of life. Living in a bad marriage is horrible. Otherwise, you wouldn't have decided to divorce. And even if you didn't initiate your divorce, you know in your heart that you deserve to be married to someone who wants to be married to you, not someone who's staying around because he feels guilty about leaving. We have all seen the dark side of divorce, but it doesn't have to be that way. By using what you learn in this book, you can be part of the solution.

Peaceful divorce sounds like an oxymoron, but it's a concept whose time has come. People have started to figure out that divorce does not have to be bitter, nasty, and punitive. Many couples are looking for ways to end the "home wreckonomics" approach to divorcing. The legal field is slowly rising to meet this demand with mediation and collaborative law, but you can have a peaceful divorce that redefines your family without relying on lawyers or the legal system to provide the answers for you. Quality legal and financial advice can be useful, but you don't need a lawyer to teach you how to keep peace in your family and resolve conflicts. If you have the will, this book will give you many ways. You can look at conflict as an opportunity to fix things that needed fixing and to change things that needed to be changed, not as a negative experience to be avoided.

Divorce is one solution to living in an unhappy, unfulfilling marriage. But your divorce doesn't begin and end with the legal process. It's going to change your life, and you're in control of how it's going to do that. The choices you make will define what your life looks like afterward. Scary, yes. But it's also okay to allow yourself to look at this time in your life as a new adventure. If you are divorcing so you can be happier, it's okay to start being happy *now* and find some bittersweet joy in your decision to let each other go. If you're divorcing because your spouse wants to get divorced, it's important to learn from what went wrong and to make the best of the situation.

This book will teach you everything you need to know to

renegotiate and redefine your relationship with your spouse, put an end to unproductive arguments and behaviors, negotiate a fair, win-win settlement, and move on from your marriage happy, healthy, and whole.

You will learn:

- How to create a divorce mission statement

- Why marriages end and why yours ended

- 8 simple tools to resolve family conflict

- 8 ways to keep yourself sane no matter what

- How to set your personal GPS to goodness and keep it there

- How to figure out what you want and how to get it

- How to walk your talk all the time

- How to grieve the end of your marriage

- How to forgive yourself and your spouse and accept your divorce

- How to negotiate successfully to get what you want and what you need

- How to come out of your divorce a better person

You can do this. This isn't rocket science and it isn't magic. A lot of it is simply common sense. The key is *you* have to do it. No one is coming to save you—except for you.

The good news is that if you keep using what you learn in this book throughout your divorce and in your new life afterward, you will be happier than you are today. Your children will be better off and may even tell you they understand why you divorced. You will comprehend and be at peace with the money and property you receive in your settlement. You won't cling to long-standing grudges. You will have insight and peacemaking skills that will prepare you to be more successful in your next relationship. You will be ready to love again.

At the end of your divorce, you will be proud of how you handled it. You'll be proud that you served as a role model for your children and your community. You'll have the satisfaction of knowing that you've done the right thing, behaved in line with your values, and made the best of an unfortunate situation . . . contrasted with others who instead choose fighting for the sake of fighting, taking the low road, and then realizing the price of all of that too late.

Together, we can change the course of how divorce is handled in our culture. It's time for peaceful divorce to be the new status quo. If you help pave the way, everyone who divorces will have an easier go of it. Imagine how much family grief could be eliminated if dissolving a marriage meant keeping the peace and embracing the change rather than tearing families apart.

The first step is to decide what you want at the end of this process and to spell it out. You'll need to set goals at the outset so you'll be able to stay on course when things aren't going your way. There will be temptation to behave badly during your divorce. Your mission statement will keep you focused.

Divorce Mission Statement

A mission statement for your divorce is your compass guiding you away from conflict and toward peace. There is a huge distinction between what's important and what's urgent. We're often drawn toward the next most urgent thing, but often it's really not important, at least not to the goals you've set for yourself. There will be many tempting distractions during your divorce. Your mission statement will keep you on track.

LAURA AND ANDY'S DIVORCE MISSION STATEMENT

Laura and Andy divorced three years into their marriage, when their son John was two years old. Laura asked for the divorce. Andy thought their marriage was fine and was very embarrassed that his young bride wanted to leave him, especially so early on. Andy had a lot of anger, which Laura was able to meet with compassion. She saw signs before her wedding that she wasn't going to be happy with Andy, yet she didn't have the courage to call it off. She felt like she owed him the decency of handling their divorce with respect and collaboration after having failed to be honest about her feelings before the wedding.

Laura wrote out her divorce mission statement in her notebook and showed it to Andy:

At the end of my divorce it will be true that John has two supportive parents, committed to co-parenting, our financial responsibility was divided fairly, and I value what I learned about myself during my divorce and it made me a better person. I'll do this by putting John's best interests above my own, focusing on accepting situations rather than manipulating outcomes, and allowing myself time to grieve. As a result I will feel hopeful that I will find love again, confident that I can adjust my lifestyle to my new financial situation, and courageous about facing challenges.

Although Andy was still reeling from the news that Laura wanted to get divorced, he read her divorce mission statement and agreed with most of it. He even added a few goals of his own.

He kept a copy of it folded up in his wallet so that when he was tempted to lash out at her, or keep John away from Laura as punishment, he was able to keep his end goals in mind.

Andy appreciated his wife for seeing his side and letting him show her his pain. They agreed to live in the same town until their son was eighteen so they could effectively co-parent. Andy remarried within two years and had three more children. A few years later, Laura met a divorced man with a son John's age and they agreed to date long-distance until their children were both eighteen and then get married. They are now engaged.

Andy and Laura's son, John, went off to college this year. They both dropped him off at his dorm, along with their stepfamilies. As they were leaving, John looked at his parents and said, "I am so glad you guys were married because you had me, but for the life of me I don't know what you two saw in each other!" Everyone burst out laughing.

YOUR DIVORCE MISSION STATEMENT

As you start your divorce, life can get chaotic. You could easily end up spending your days with activities that seem to require your immediate attention but which have nothing to do with your short- or long-term goals. When you take the time to think about and craft a mission statement that suits you, it keeps you on track, which reduces stress and suffering. It points you in the direction of living in a way that you know will make you proud of yourself.

Living your mission doesn't necessarily mean a complete overhaul of your personality. Don't get bogged down in thinking you could've saved your marriage had you done something like this earlier. You're doing it now, and that's what counts. The past is the past and it doesn't matter now how you got here. If how you got here is of real concern to you, consider addressing the issue with a professional counselor, your doctor, or a support group. This is about moving forward and making sure your thoughts and behavior are in line with what you deeply care about. This will make it much easier and much less scary to let go of things that pull you off track.

If your spouse is willing to work on a mission statement with you, do it together. If not, write it on your own and consider sharing it. Your divorce mission statement should focus on your core values for dissolving your marriage and living your life afterward.

You can use the following ideas to help you write your divorce mission statement in your notebook. They are intended as a guide only, and we encourage you to make your mission statement as personal as possible. To begin, read through the ideas and choose the ones that resonate most with your core values. Choose as many as you'd like. You can use the ideas to write your own divorce mission statement, customized to fit your own situation.

At the end of my divorce, I want the following to be true:

- I was kind and honest throughout the entire process.

- My children have two supportive parents committed to co-parenting.

- We did not have to go to court to settle our divorce.

- We spent as little money as possible on our divorce, preserving assets to be split between us instead of using them to pay lawyers.

- Our financial responsibility was divided fairly.

- I still respect my former spouse and our relationship is friendly, cordial, and civil.

- I realize my marriage was not a complete mistake and value the years I was with my spouse.

- Our children understand and are reminded that our divorce is not their fault.

- I am committed to being cooperative and respectful when my spouse engages with the world as a single person (dating, working, making new friends, etc.).

- I took responsibility for any feelings of abandonment, rejection, fear, anger, grief, and guilt I had, without blaming or shaming my spouse.

I will make sure that the above statements are realized by doing the following:

- I will ask for advice from people who are a positive influence, and then follow that advice.

- I will put my children's best interests above my own.

- I will take care of myself physically and emotionally.

- I will forgive myself and my spouse for getting divorced.

- I will focus on moving forward rather than getting bogged down in the past.

- I will accept situations rather than manipulating outcomes.

- I will focus on what is important, both short term and long term.

- I will use written goals and journaling to track my progress.

- I will not use my divorce to punish myself or my spouse.

- I will not consider divorce as something that I need to recover from, but rather as something I can heal through.

Now, using the example Laura wrote in her notebook, and the ideas that resonate with you from the lists, write up your own divorce mission statement in your notebook. Refine it a few times until it feels right to you. You may even want to copy it out of your notebook so you can keep it in several places and refer to it often.

Do you see how writing out your mission statement will help you keep your actions in line with your goals? Once you've pinpointed what's most important to you, it will be easier to make sure that the most important things are accomplished.

You may want to rewrite this mission statement periodically and reassess your goals throughout the process. That's not only okay, it's encouraged. Life is a work in progress. You will change a lot during this process, and embracing the change in a positive way will help insure that you emerge happy, healthy, and whole.

Your divorce mission statement will serve as a reminder of who you want to be at the end of your divorce. Keep it handy. You will need these reminders when things get tough. The hard work of staying in touch with your mission, and realigning your behaviors to fit with your mission, will be worth it.

Creating your divorce mission statement is a huge first step, so take the time to congratulate and reward yourself. You actually wrote down your core values and are headed toward them. Rally yourself to forge ahead. You can do this, and we'll be with you every step of the way.

In chapter 3, you will learn the 8 keys to resolving family conflict. This will give you a toolbox that you can start to use *right away* to keep you moving toward peace. You will be more prepared to deal with conflict the very next time it arises in your family life.

CHAPTER 2

Why Marriages End

Many people bear adversity, very few contempt.

—PROVERB

You hear a lot about the reasons marriages end. Usually, fingers point to affairs or money. But marriages don't end because of events. In twenty years of practice, we have found that divorce occurs when two people, for whatever reason, have turned from each other and looked for satisfaction outside of the marriage. We call this *turning*.

If you are the one who asked for your divorce, it may be clear to you why your marriage is ending. If you are the still-loving partner and didn't want the divorce, as you look back, the signs that led up to your spouse wanting a divorce will become clearer to you as you reflect. Marriages fall apart through something like erosion. The breakdown starts slowly and proceeds with one tiny misstep after another, until the sum of these becomes so large that the relationship collapses.

This chapter will help you identify the series of imperceptibly small turns that led to one or both of you ultimately being so dissatisfied that the decision was made to end the marriage. Looking back at the deterioration of your marriage takes courage. But understanding what happens to typical couples, and what happened to you, can help normalize the situation for you, and this will allow you to move on. If you initiated the divorce, you'll have a more clear understanding of why. And if you didn't, the process will help you appreciate that this isn't a sudden, single event that could have been prevented. Turning happened before either of you saw the signs or understood their gravity.

Though the particulars vary from couple to couple, there is a predictable sequence of events that occurs as a marriage breaks down. While you're in it, it's difficult or even impossible to see. As outsiders, we can identify the turns—when he turned into a workaholic and she turned to redecorating the house, or when he spent all of his time coaching baseball and she spent hers lobbying for a promotion. When spouses turn outside the marriage for satisfaction, it's not always to drugs and sex. Often it's something innocuous or even something positive, like working hard or focusing on the kids. But it's turning all the same.

Satisfaction Wanes

The first stage of the breakdown occurs when one or both spouses realize that they are not getting a need met by the marriage. The nature of the need isn't as important as the fact that it's not getting met. And this is how the erosion of a marriage starts.

When you got married, your relationship probably met the needs that were important to you: affection, sexual fulfillment, conversation, fun and recreation, honesty and openness, physical attractiveness, financial and domestic support, family commitment, and mutual admiration.

But as time went on, you let things slip. You stopped dressing up and you went out less and less. Maybe you quit talking so much. Let's face it, that's the way most relationships work. Then you reached a tipping point but probably didn't realize it, at least not at the time. And if your spouse initiated the divorce, you *really* didn't realize it. Or if you did suspect, maybe it was too hard to face. Humans have a remarkable capacity for denial.

Turning is insidious and incremental, like erosion. If you'd seen it coming, either of you might have been able to stop it. Maybe you saw a glimmer, but you didn't know what it was or how damaging it could be. *Turning happens, and it's nobody's fault.*

If spouses aren't getting their needs met within the marriage, sometimes complaining and conflict begin in an effort to get what they want from their partner: "Why do you go golfing every Sunday morning with your friends when I have asked you for weeks to play tennis with me and you say you are too tired?"

Plenty of couples fight from time to time. Healthy arguing can be a valid and effective way for many couples to solve problems. Conflict alone doesn't indicate that a marriage is headed for divorce. Some couples even enjoy fighting and making up.

Forget fighting. It is very unlikely to be the real issue. Couples get into trouble because they can't resolve how to help each other get their needs met. At this point, the fights may involve a lot of blaming and shaming. "You always go to bed two hours before I do so we aren't having sex during the week anymore," she says. "Yeah, well, if you worked, I wouldn't have to put in all this overtime and be so exhausted," he counters. The fight is a red herring, but it does give valuable clues to what's really going on, even if it's not the issue that is stated.

Think of the argument above. She's complaining that he goes to bed too early, but what she's really saying is "You aren't paying any attention to me anymore." His response blames her for not working, but what he's really saying is "I feel so much pressure to earn money that I don't have any energy left over for anything else. Help me!" But because of the blame, shame, and guilt overtones, this couple doesn't hear each other's real concerns, and as a result, they each fail to communicate what the other really needs to hear. If her statement had been "I am so lonely. I love you so much and I miss you because you work all the time," and if his statement had been "I miss you, too, but I feel like our budget is out of control. I feel so much pressure to earn money. I hate this as much as you do, maybe more. What can we do?" *Who on earth would not respond to this kind of communication?*

While you may have missed the opportunities in your marriage to establish real communication, there is value in understanding where those little missteps occurred that ultimately pushed you over the cliff.

Both spouses may feel misunderstood. Each individual may be dissatisfied about a different need. If both spouses in the example above wanted to spend more time together, they could work on a mutual plan to save money; they could agree to find ways to be thrifty. Or if a couple wanted to be more physically attractive for each other, they could spend time at the gym, go to a healthful cooking class, or shop for new clothes together.

Couples who can't resolve their fights may think they have conflicting values. One wants more financial security, but the other wants to buy expensive electronics while they can still afford it, before they have children. They may have the same values, family first and financial security, but they have a different way of thinking about how to go about it. But because they never scratch the surface of the conflict, they don't even realize they're actually on the same page.

When one spouse feels frustrated because one of his needs is not being met, he may be tempted to punish the other spouse (consciously or subconsciously) by withholding and refusing to satisfy the other's needs. As the cycle of frustration and dissatisfaction continues, each partner keeps asking the other for the same thing over and over again in different ways but never gets it. Both feel misunderstood and can't see a way to break through.

Compulsion Begins

People need what they need. In an unsatisfying marriage, either spouse can deny those needs for only so long and then will feel a compulsion to meet them wherever they can be met. Sometimes people act out; other times they just shut down and get depressed. Marital depression can manifest in countless ways: not engaging in conversation, falling asleep on the couch to avoid sleeping together, losing interest in activities the two of you used to enjoy, stopping displays of affection, forgetting an anniversary, making snarky comments, leaving messes for the other to clean up, or bad grooming, just to name a few. The shut-down and depressed spouse often feels worried, hopeless, and scared because she doesn't know what to do about it.

When acting out begins, a couple's problems surface and are "acted out" in daily living. Take Kent and Nancy for example. They were married eight years when they hit a rough patch and their marriage began to deteriorate.

Kent wished his wife Nancy would be more honest with him about her thoughts and feelings. He asked her opinion on current events and she said she didn't know. He wondered what she thought of a movie they'd seen and she told him it was "good." Kent tried to draw her out through probing questions, but she didn't engage with him.

Kent began to pick fights with Nancy, hoping that a spirited conversation might make her more communicative. She shut down even more. Kent asked her just to spend time talking with him over a glass of wine at the end of the day. She became self-conscious and defensive and yelled at him for trying to make her look dumb.

Kent was desperate for a connection through the sharing of ideas, which was completely absent from his marriage. One day, at the local coffee shop he overheard two women debating politics and was instantly riveted.

The following week, Kent returned to the coffee shop and noticed one of the women from the week before sitting on a couch reading. Kent was excited as he sat down next to her and asked if she was enjoying her book. They spent the next half hour talking about literature.

It was just a friendly conversation. However, when Kent went home to Nancy that evening, he saw her as even more dull and unexciting than he had before. Kent had begun to turn outside his marriage to get his need for open communication and engaging conversation met. A distraction appeared on his radar screen that fed an underlying hunger. He had begun to resent his wife for what she was not giving him. His marriage had begun to unravel. This is how innocently and simply turning begins.

The Four Horsemen of the Apocalypse

Once a relationship has started to turn, four attitudes present themselves as common preludes to divorce: criticism, defensiveness, contempt, and stonewalling. Dr. John Gottman, a psychologist at the University of Washington and author of *10 Lessons to Transform Your Marriage*, calls these attitudes the "Four Horsemen of the Apocalypse." In his study of more than two thousand couples over two decades, he discovered that the presence of these attitudes in a marriage could be used to predict which couples would divorce with 94 percent accuracy.

We worked with Nancy and Kent (not their real names, of course) a few years ago in mediation. They are, sadly, typical of how criticism, defensiveness, contempt, and stonewalling lead to turning. As you'll see, their turning started innocently and built up imperceptibly over time. By the time we did their mediation, though, these events had distilled into a complete marital breakdown and we saw the gravity of these seemingly unimportant transactions immediately. We've changed some of the details and filled in some of the dialogue for the purposes of this illustration.

CRITICISM

After his conversation at the coffee shop, Kent began to attack Nancy's character. "You are so boring," he told her. "You never have anything to say. Don't you have any opinions about anything? Don't you care what's going on in the world?"

Kent was making Nancy wrong for being who she is. This made him feel entitled to engage in stimulating conversation with other women wherever and whenever he felt like it. He was more cavalier in his turning. Soon, he started striking up conversations with random women in the bookstore, at the grocery, and at work. In addition to feeling entitled, however, Kent also felt guilty for being mean to his wife. His guilty feelings caused him to be even more critical of her. He pigeonholed her as the type of person who has nothing to say. His marriage was now on shaky ground.

DEFENSIVENESS

Nancy was irritated by Kent's critical words. She felt victimized and wanted him to stop haranguing her. She was walking on eggshells in her own house and started to use a variety of tactics to defend herself from his disapproval.

Nancy made excuses for her lack of communication with Kent. "I never said I was an intellectual! Why are you grilling me about politics? I told you I never really cared about stuff like that."

Sick of being picked on, Nancy had a litany of cross complaints about Kent's shortcomings: "I may not know anything about independent films, but you are a slob. Who cares how smart you are when you'd be living in a pigsty if it weren't for me cleaning up after you?"

Nancy also found herself whining at Kent: "It's not fair that you have all of these expectations for what should interest me. I'm happy with my art projects and decorating around the house. Stop trying to fix me!"

Angry with Kent, Nancy began to spend more time in the evenings in the basement with her watercolors. She felt unaccepted by Kent for being herself and signed up for a still life painting class at the community college. Both Kent *and* Nancy had turned.

CONTEMPT

When Nancy reached the point of contempt with Kent, she could no longer contain herself. One evening he got up from his computer and she saw that he had left his email account open. She looked at it and saw several emails from another woman and went berserk.

"You're cheating on me online! I *knew* you were sitting here pretending to be working while you were really talking to some other woman. I spend every day making a nice place for us to live, and this is how you repay me?"

Nancy found it impossible to relate to Kent in any way other than with hostility. She began mocking and insulting him on a daily basis, rolling her eyes whenever he spoke. Their relationship was now in crisis.

Whether contempt is expressed openly or suggested through

subtle body language like dismissive eye rolling or sneering, once it is expressed there's a very high risk of the marriage ending in divorce.

Contempt differs from other types of anger. A husband who feels contempt for his wife has elevated himself to a level above her. A contemptuous wife thinks her husband is no longer worthy of her love because he is beneath her. Contempt is hierarchical, where garden variety anger isn't.

A critical statement toward a spouse might be "You always choose where we eat dinner on Friday nights. You don't care at all about what I like to eat." Contempt contains more disgust: "You are such a selfish pig. All you want to do is stuff yourself at the pizza buffet. You could care less about what I want. You're such a loser." Contempt indicates complete rejection. If both people in a marriage have come to the point that they feel contempt toward each other, it is very difficult to recover.

STONEWALLING

Sick of the fighting and unsure of what to do, Kent and Nancy both began stonewalling. Kent found the intellectual stimulation he was seeking on the Internet. Nancy spent more and more time painting. Their fighting was replaced with silence. They rarely ate meals together. Nancy wouldn't make eye contact with Kent and answered his halfhearted attempts to engage her with simple one-word answers.

Kent's online chats changed into outright flirting. He became obsessed with a woman named Mary whom he met posting on an author's blog, and checked his email addictively for messages from her. When Nancy came into his office and asked what he was doing, he'd minimize his computer screen and change the subject.

Nancy suspected Kent was cheating on her or was about to. When she caught him minimizing his computer screen, she rolled her eyes and sneered at him. She was full of rage and ready to blow a gasket.

Within a few weeks, Nancy filed for divorce from Kent. He was shocked at first and thought she was leaving him because of the email relationship he was having with Mary. But Mary was just the last straw after each of the Four Horsemen of the Apocalypse rode into Kent and Nancy's marriage. It's seldom just one problem or significant event that destroys a marriage. Marriages erode over time. Sometimes the reasons why can be only seen in hindsight. It can be painful and it takes courage to look at where you turned away from your marriage. But now as you rebuild your life, you have a chance to get your needs met in a way that doesn't hurt your spouse any more.

Turning: Kent's Story

In an effort to understand why he was divorcing, Kent used the prompts that appear in the next section and wrote in his notebook to reflect on his marriage. He started with what he considered the last straw and worked back in time to identify where criticism, defensiveness, contempt, and stonewalling showed up. He thought understanding how things fell apart would be a big part of him being able to let go and move on. The following is an entry from his notebook:

The last straw for Nancy and I was when I met Mary online. Mary and I had such a great time writing to each other it was almost an addiction for me. I couldn't wait to read her emails and checked for them constantly. Nancy is right, I did have an emotional affair with her. I'd like to say that is what ended our marriage because that would give me a nice, neat reason. But the truth is, Nancy and I were in trouble long before I met Mary online. Nancy and I were living more as roommates than husband and wife for at least the last six months of our marriage.

Leading up to that, Nancy and I were really horrible to each other. It wasn't just basic arguing about who was right about something or being irritated with each other's little habits. We were downright mean. We called each other names. We knew exactly what buttons to push and I know for sure some of the things I said to her were devastating. Her meanness toward me didn't hurt as much, I think, because I had Mary to lean on. So while I was trashing Nancy, Mary was building me up.

We were living separate lives and we knew it. On some level I think I felt so bad about how boring I thought she was that I had to pick on her to justify my actions. Then, Nancy would get defensive. We started a vicious cycle.

I knew who Nancy was when I married her. It was fine for a while, and then I just became bored. It's like I couldn't help myself. I was desperate for someone to talk to and if it wasn't going to be her, it was going to be someone else. I didn't set out to ruin my marriage by talking to other women, but as I look back now I can see how one thing led to another.

Turning: Your Story

Can you see through the example of Kent and Nancy that the breakdown of your marriage was probably not just one event? Take time to reflect on the erosion of your own marriage.

On a new page in your notebook, write the story of the turning in your marriage. Start with what you consider the main cause of your divorce, the straw that broke the camel's back, and work backward in time. How and when did criticism, defensiveness, contempt, and stonewalling appear in your relationship? If you don't feel like writing entire paragraphs like Kent did, jot down your ideas in a list. Come back and fill it in with more detail later if you feel like it. The idea is to come up with a general framework of these behaviors, to see where things truly started to fall apart and how each small erosion or turn ultimately contributed to that final event. You'll begin to see the sum of the events, big and small, of the past years or months that led you and your spouse to divorce. This is not to humiliate you, but to set you free and allow you to move toward acceptance.

Next, we'll ask you to examine your own role in the breakdown of your marriage so you can see where you personally turned. Keep in mind the goal of this is not to blame or punish you! The purpose of looking back is not about a remedy or wishing you could go back and repair your marriage. It is about accepting your responsibility and gaining perspective.

Accepting Responsibility: Where Did I Fall Short?

One way to let your spouse off the hook and help you let go is to look at the ways in which you contributed to the breakdown of your marriage by falling short as a partner. It's important for you to take responsibility for your role in the erosion of your marriage because *that is where your power is.* You can only change you.

The purpose of gaining this insight is to help you move past patently blaming your spouse for all your problems so you can see him or her in a better light. Also, understanding where you became weak as a partner provides a lesson from your marriage. If you strengthen yourself in the areas where you were weak, you will be a more attractive partner in your next relationship. If you don't take the time to learn where you went wrong, you are at risk for repeating the same patterns.

Some of the turning that occurs in a marriage is because one or both partners have lost their attraction to each other. No matter what we each need individually to be attracted to someone and feel compatible with them, there are certain general attributes that make a marriage satisfying and sustainable. There are also certain attributes that can make a spouse unattractive over time, no matter how much passion was present in the beginning. Frankly stated, there are some things people do and ways they act that make them fall short as a partner *especially* in a marriage.

Ways We May Fall Short

The following are characteristics that spouses may exhibit toward each other that can weaken their attraction to each other, and some questions you can ask yourself to discern whether any of them describe you. Since you can't change your spouse, for our purposes here, do not do your spouse's inventory. As you consider the following, focus on where you fell short, so you can learn and move on.

CARETAKING

Did your spouse have to take care of you or did you each hold your own? Did you do your fair share around the household? Did you contribute financially through earning income or managing the family budget? Did you relate to your spouse as an equal, adult partner? Did you relate to your spouse more like a child or a sibling sometimes? Do you feel like you need your spouse to keep up your lifestyle, even though you know you are not happy in the relationship?

LOW SELF-WORTH

How do you define yourself outside of your marriage? Do you feel good about your life even though you are going through a challenging time right now? Did you rely on your spouse for encouragement and reassurance in a way that you know was annoying? Do you feel needy? Are you making sure you are taking time to soothe and care for yourself during this difficult transition?

REPRESSION

Did you share your emotions with your spouse? Did you say "I love you" in your marriage? Do you feel comfortable with the full range of your feelings? Did you hold back from your spouse? Do you feel like the two of you were once close but then, at some point, you pulled away? If so, why? Have you noticed a need to express yourself in a way you haven't up to now?

OBSESSION

Was there something you were preoccupied by that you couldn't help engaging with? Did you ever feel annoyed by your spouse if she interfered with your obsession? Keep in mind this could be anything: food, gambling, TV, sports, shopping, etc. It could also be something that seems positive and beneficial, like volunteer work, coaching the kids, or working hard for a promotion. What drove you to distraction?

CONTROLLING

Did you try to control your spouse's behavior? Did you check up on your spouse's whereabouts? Did you get angry when your spouse didn't do what you told him to do? Did you nag? Were you childlike to get your way? Did you ever feel more like a parent toward your spouse than an equal partner, even though you may have resented it? Were you annoyed or angry when your spouse didn't act like you wanted?

DENIAL

Did you hide things from your spouse even if she confronted you directly about them? Do you have debt that your spouse doesn't know about? Did you tell your spouse you stopped doing something that you continued behind his back? When your spouse points out something you do that's annoying, do you deny it? Do you try with cross complaints to defuse situations where you feel your spouse is accusing you of something?

POOR COMMUNICATION

Did you talk to your spouse? Did you listen to your spouse? Did you share things with her that she needed to know to function well in your family? Did you remind your spouse of important dates and help keep his life running smoothly? Have you ever not told your spouse something important as a punishment or because you didn't think you had to?

WEAK BOUNDARIES

Did you feel overextended in your marriage? Did you say yes to your spouse's requests when you'd rather have said no? Did you give your spouse privacy? Did you feel like it was your right to go through your spouse's personal belongings without her knowing or without her permission?

LACK OF TRUST

Are you hiding anything from your spouse (a credit card, relationship, habit, etc.) that he would be surprised to discover about you? Have you cheated on your spouse without him knowing? Have you lied to your spouse? Have you kept up appearances in a situation that is basically fake?

ANGER

Did you feel angry toward your spouse and act out by yelling, fighting, or being passive-aggressive? Did she know you were mad and why? Did you know you were mad and why? Are you still angry? How long have you been angry? Have you ever tried to deal with the source of your frustration and solve the problem or are you just mad? Has your anger made you unpleasant to be around?

SEXUAL PROBLEMS

Did you have a good sex life in your marriage? If not, was it ever good? When did it change? What made it unsatisfying? Did you ever try to talk about it with your spouse? How did that go? Was there an affair in your marriage? If so, what would help you move past it, even though you are divorcing now?

CHEMICAL DEPENDENCY

Did you self-medicate with alcohol or prescription or illegal drugs? Do you think you have a substance abuse problem? Did your drinking or drug use contribute to your divorce? Do you need help? Has anyone told you recently that they are worried about you partying too much? Have you missed work or other important events because you've been out late or are hungover? If you think you have a problem with drugs or alcohol, please seek treatment before you try to deal with the many complicated issues involved in a divorce.

Having the courage to look at the way you exhibited these and other unflattering characteristics in your marriage is not for the weak of heart. But if you can do it, the understanding you will gain will help you be a lot more compassionate toward yourself and your spouse as well as help you move forward beyond shame and guilt. As an added bonus, if you choose to work on the areas you identify, it will help you as you enter into new relationships. You may be tempted to think that you wouldn't have acted in any of these ways if only you were getting what you needed from your spouse. Don't fall into that. Remember, this exercise is about responsibility. It doesn't matter *why* you did it. It's only important that you understand that these dynamics were present and were your contribution to the breakdown. You must acknowledge them and accept responsibility before you can use what you have learned to make your divorce process more restorative than damaging.

Right now, you might not think you exhibited any of these characteristics. However, as you use what you learn in this book, you may realize something new about yourself.

Where Did I Fall Short? Tanya's Story

Tanya was married to Edward for thirteen years when they decided to divorce. Tanya was committed to looking at where she fell short in her marriage, so she read through the characteristics that can weaken attraction in marriage and thought about how she exhibited them in her relationship with Edward. The following is an entry from her notebook. Writing this up helped her come to terms with the ways she acted toward Edward that weakened his attraction to her. It was not easy, but Tanya was glad she did it and for the insight she gained. It helped give her closure.

Edward took care of me so many ways, both financially and emotionally. He handled all the money and made so many of the decisions about keeping us within budget that it put him more in the role of being a father to me than a partner.

This was due partly to my low self-worth. Though I appeared confident on the outside, I needed a lot of reassurance from Edward. I fished for compliments and asked if he liked how I looked or what I was wearing in a way that I know he found annoying.

Edward was more excited about life than I was. I loved this about him at first and then became jealous about it later. I felt weird about his joy so much sometimes that I withheld positive emotion from him simply because I was uncomfortable and didn't know how to express it.

I was obsessed with food and dieting which made sharing meals together hard on Edward. If I was even just a few pounds over my goal weight or missed workouts, I felt fat and ugly and withheld affection from him because I didn't want him to touch me. I also ruined a lot of nice meals by calling our foods disgustingly fattening or bad even though they were delicious and Edward was fine with my body.

I'm a clean freak. Edward is definitely clean but more relaxed about the normal clutter of day-to-day living. I nagged at him constantly to put his belongings where I thought they should go which made me seem more like a controlling mother than his wife.

Sometimes when I wanted to have the upper hand with Edward, I wouldn't tell him things that would have made it easier on him to share. Like, if I knew it was his mom's birthday and he may forget to call her, I'd just let that happen rather than reminding him. I played games like expecting him to be a mind reader. I acted like I thought he should know what I wanted from him to make me happy rather than just telling him.

One of the things that really drove him nuts was that I was a very good friend to my girlfriends so he knew I was capable of thoughtfulness. At times I think my sister knew more about what was going on in our marriage than my husband did.

Though I never cheated on Edward, I wasn't completely trustworthy either. I have a credit card right now that I still haven't told him about with a $3,000 balance on it.

Part of the reason I have hidden things from Edward and been a poor communicator is because I know I have issues with my anger. Sometimes I don't even know where my anger comes from and I'm afraid if I begin to express it, I will completely lose control.

One of the most dissatisfying parts of our marriage has been our sex life. It's embarrassing to admit but we barely had one. We had sex once every couple of weeks and I felt like I was doing it as a favor to him. I had gotten to the point where I didn't even care about whether it was pleasing to me.

Though neither of us drank or did drugs, I did take a prescription sedative almost every night which I told my doctor I needed for anxiety but I really think now it was a way for me to numb out and get through my evenings with Edward and not really feel how sad and desperate I was in our marriage.

Where Did I Fall Short? Your Story

Can you see from Tanya's entry how she reflected on each of the characteristics that weaken attraction in marriage and then wrote about how they showed up in her behavior toward Edward? Now it is your turn to do the same thing. This is not for the weak of heart, but you can do it!

Get out your notebook and contemplate the characteristics that may have weakened your marriage.

Which of these apply to you? What comes to mind when you ask yourself the questions? If you don't want to write in a story format, like Tanya did, simply jot down some notes. You may also want to number the traits according to which was most predominant. Writing in your notebook about where you fell short is intended to help you discover for yourself where you may have contributed to the turning that eroded your relationship. The idea is not to lay blame or hurt you. It is to help you take responsibility for your part of the breakdown. For each characteristic, decide if it applied to you in your marriage. If it was an issue, write about it.

You may even think of other things that made you unattractive to your spouse. Write them up like Tanya did. Revisit this in your notebook later and you may see things differently. Remember that the idea isn't to make you appear wrong. The goal is for you to realize that it takes two to divorce, and to give you the opportunity to understand why your marriage is ending, so you can set goals for yourself in your new life, which we will guide you to do in chapter 6, "What You Want Now."

Why Are You Leaving Your Marriage?
Unmet Needs

Now that you have reflected on the series of events (turning) that resulted in the end of your marriage, and where you fell short, the next step is to identify the needs that you expected to have met in your marriage but which somehow got left by the wayside.

Along with identifying your unmet needs, it is important to understand *how* they went unmet in your marriage and describe the void and ultimately *where you turned outside your marriage to get the need met*. Remember that cheating isn't the only way couples turn. Turning can manifest as behaviors that would be healthy if they weren't contributing to the erosion of your marriage. For example, working hard for long hours can be a fantastic way to earn money and get ahead. In a healthy marriage, spouses can support each other through a period where one or both of them is putting in extra hours as long as they find the situation satisfactory. However, when a spouse is staying late at work as a way to avoid going home, it's turning.

MARITAL NEEDS

Some of the most common needs that couples expect to have met in their marriages are:

- Affection and sexual fulfillment

- Conversation

- Fun and recreation

- Honesty and openness

- Physical attractiveness

- Financial support

- Domestic support

- Family commitment

- Mutual admiration

Unmet Needs: Mark's Story

Mark was married to Deborah for twelve years. He'd had what he called a mild midlife crisis when, at age forty-one, he decided to ask Deborah for a divorce. Mark had simply had enough. All he knew for sure was he wasn't happy with Deborah and he wanted a drastic change, even if it meant lowering his standard of living. He felt trapped and just wanted out, but he wasn't sure exactly why until he reflected on it and wrote in his notebook. To discover why his marriage ended, Mark thought about each of the common needs couples have in their marriages and exactly how he was dissatisfied. In his notebook, Mark wrote up what he needed from Deborah that he wasn't getting and how he turned outside his marriage in an attempt to get the needs met. Then he wrote about what he needed for his new life since he was divorcing. His intention was not to use the information to blame Deborah for the erosion of their marriage. He wanted to be able to use it to set goals for his new future.

> Affection and sexual fulfillment were good for the first five years of our marriage and then waned and became nonexistent. I sought affection from my female friends and enjoyed their hugs and positive comments. I often fantasized about having sex with other women even while having sex with Deborah. Right now I need time alone without the complications of worrying about my sex life. I'm very confused and sad.
>
> Deborah and I both let our physical attractiveness slide. We met when we were both young and skinny, but over the years we developed bad eating habits and the pounds crept on. I felt like Deborah let special grooming habits that she did for me when we were lovers go by the wayside once the kids were born. I stopped feeling attractive to her because I've gained twenty pounds and got my need to feel attractive met anywhere and

everywhere. I love to flirt and did so shamelessly with whoever was willing. I really needed affirmation that I've still got it even in middle age. What I need now is to make health and fitness a part of my daily life rather than a to do list item which never gets done. I also need to focus on getting my self-esteem from myself and stop flirting, so I can gain real confidence rather than relying on shallow compliments to make me feel good.

Financial support was really unbalanced in our marriage. Deborah has a much higher paying job than I do. She resented me sometimes because she doesn't think I worked hard enough to earn up to my full potential. I also felt more like her child than her husband when I had to ask her for money. I need to be with someone who feels like working isn't everything.

Deborah insisted on being in charge of our house and didn't want any domestic support from me at all. I felt like I was one of the children. I didn't know where anything was in the house. If Deborah heard me looking for something, she'd ask me what I needed and get it for me. Our house was so immaculate that it didn't feel like home to me. I need to set up a household for myself where I can feel totally comfortable and let things get a little messy, leave my bed unmade and let dishes sit in the sink once in a while. I want my children to be able to leave their toys out without getting yelled at.

Unmet Needs: Your Story

Now it is your turn to see where the needs you expected to have met in your marriage went unfulfilled. After a while, perhaps months or years, of not getting your needs met, you couldn't deny yourself any longer and sought to meet them outside your marriage. This could have been in the form of another person or activity. Or you could have sedated and controlled your needs through some distraction or other numbing behavior.

Like Mark did, contemplate the list of marital needs most people have. Decide which of these was going unmet in your marriage. For each one, write up how the need went unmet in your marriage. How were you dissatisfied? How did you turn or consider turning outside your marriage to try to meet the need? What are your feelings associated with not getting your need met? How do you feel about having sought to meet it elsewhere? Keep in mind that this is *not about blaming your spouse for not meeting your need*. Do not fall into the temptation of thinking that your spouse alone caused your divorce. Undoubtedly, your spouse's needs weren't met either. The purpose of writing down your unmet needs is to help you understand why your marriage ended, so you can eventually move into acceptance and set goals for your future.

In your notebook, write up whatever comes to mind, either as a story, like Mark did, or simply jot down your ideas.

Once you realize that turning outside your marriage to get your needs met caused your marriage to dissolve over time, you can let go of the myth that the breakdown was one catastrophic event. The value to hold in mind is that it does you no good to blame yourself or your spouse for your divorce. Let it come as a relief that where there is no blame there should be no guilt and therefore no punishment. Understanding how you turned can help you find a new way to relate to your spouse as you redefine your family and find happiness and satisfaction as a single person.

Once you understand why you are divorcing and see your role in the process, you'll be ready to consider letting go and moving on. If you've been doing the same thing over and over in your marriage, expecting different results, it will be a relief to think about doing something entirely different and moving in a brand-new direction.

The Benefits of Making Your Divorce Work

Now that you can see there is not just one event or reason for your divorce, you can come to an understanding about why your marriage is ending. Knowing all of the reasons why you are divorcing provides you with the closure you need to say good-bye and move on. Divorce is a difficult and painful way to solve the problem of living in an unhappy marriage. However, there is a silver lining. You are now free to find the happiness your relationship lacked.

Re-read what you wrote in your notebook about your unmet needs and how you turned outside your marriage to meet them. Then, write up the benefits of making your divorce work. Many of the divorcing people we meet eventually enjoy a fresh start, even though this is something that doesn't happen immediately. Embracing the opportunity to change is something you'll come to appreciate more as time goes on.

You can view your divorce as a second chance to go back and become the person you've always dreamed you'd become before an unsatisfying marriage thwarted your goals of happiness. In his notebook, Mark, the man in the preceding example, wrote up the following benefits of his divorce:

I am so sad about my divorce but it's also a good thing in so many ways. First of all, I can get to know myself again. I feel like I lost myself under Deborah's controlling nature and I'm excited to have alone time to do what I want, even if I'm not sure what that is right now. I can go have some fun and not worry about getting yelled at for being spontaneous, loud and messy. I love talking to my sister and women in general and now I can do that without feeling sad or guilty that Deborah and I don't have that kind of connection. I can start taking care of my health and work on my fitness so I feel more attractive not just for potential new girlfriends, but for myself.

It will be such a relief to not have to go to Deborah about every little purchase I want to make. I really hated that. I also think that living in my own bachelor pad will allow me to bond with my kids because we can goof around and play together without worrying that Deborah is going to yell at us for being loud or making a mess. Mostly, I'm just excited to get a fresh start and really be who I am. I felt so sad and trapped in our marriage that I stopped really living years ago and was just getting through my days with no joy.

Writing down the benefits of your divorce may feel counter-intuitive. If you need to, start slowly by jotting down just a few things that you think will be better in your life as a result of leaving your marriage. You can come back later and add to your list once the idea of your divorce being a solution to a problem in your life begins to sink in a bit more.

Starting Your New Life

We hope you understand now that a marriage erodes over time as both spouses turn away from each other to get things they expected to get in their marriages but simply haven't. Both spouses have a role in the breakdown of a marriage. Look back at your notebook and congratulate yourself for being brave and mature enough to reflect on why your marriage dissolved, without getting bogged down on the low road of blame, shame, and guilt. Being able to look at yourself and acknowledge your role will allow you to move on and find the happiness you seek because you have made important progress in your healing.

You can begin to let go because you realize that although there are many reasons you are leaving your marriage, it is really no one's fault. You don't have to come up with someone else to blame or a reason to justify your divorce. You can let go knowing that both you and your spouse deserve to get what you want and need from a relationship and it's okay that the two of you couldn't do that for each other over the long haul.

In the next chapter, you'll learn 8 keys to resolving family conflict, which will enable you to leave your marriage gracefully. These keys will help you improve communication with your spouse and minimize conflict as you move through the divorce process and redefine your relationship.

CHAPTER 3

The 8 Keys to Resolving Family Conflict

Conflict is the beginning of consciousness.

—M. ESTHER HARDING

You never thought it would happen to you, yet here you are faced with divorce. Maybe you asked for the divorce. Maybe you're the one who is being left. Even if it is something you and your spouse both want equally, you are facing a crisis.

If divorce is your reality, why not make the best of it? This may seem impossible right now, given the state of your relationship. It is not. Even if you are not on speaking terms with your spouse today, you can end the conflict in your relationship and uncover peace.

You can learn how to bring peace into your marriage, even as it is dissolving. Peacemaking is a skill, just like any other, and it starts with understanding and using 8 keys to resolving family conflict. Keep in mind that it is actually harder to remain at odds with someone than it is to make peace.

The 8 keys take only a minute to learn, but a lifetime to master. Practice makes perfect.

The 8 Keys to Resolving Family Conflict

1. Be hard on the problem, not the people.

2. Understand that acknowledging and listening are not the same as obeying.

3. Use "I" statements.

4. Give the benefit of the doubt.

5. Have awkward conversations in real time.

6. Keep the conversation going. Life is a dialogue.

7. Ask yourself "Would I rather be happy or right?"

8. Be easy to talk to.

KEY 1. BE HARD ON THE PROBLEM, NOT THE PEOPLE

Change the nature of the fight and you'll change the dynamic. Stop throwing stones in arguments. Using blame, shame, or guilt to get your spouse to do something will become less effective as your relationship ends, because each of you will stop making the little concessions you once made for each other in the relationship. Instead, address the problem rather than laying blame on your spouse. For example, "Whether or not to sell our house is a tough decision; we both have a lot of work to do, and I would like to work together to figure this out" works much better than "If you'd only earned more money while we were married, we wouldn't have to think about selling our house."

If you don't keep the problem separate from your relationship, you risk having the conflict overtake your life (especially *after* your divorce). When two people who are stakeholders in a relationship are at odds, they sometimes say and do all sorts of irrational things, project, deny, and shift blame.

All this drama has nothing to do with solving your problem. But there are things you can do to focus hard on the problem, not the person. The goal is to work *with* your spouse, rather than being adversarial.

- **Bite your tongue.** Think before you respond. Those few seconds of tongue biting can save you a lot of trouble in the long run.

- **Remember that your problem is mutual.** You need your spouse in order to solve this problem—and to reach an agreement. You will catch more flies with honey than with vinegar.

- **It takes two to have an argument.** If you refuse to take the bait for a fight, the fight can't happen.

- **Reframe your problem as a mutual problem and use "we" language.** "We need to decide what to do with the credit card debt" gets a different reception than "You need to deal with your credit card debt or we'll never have an agreement."

- **Think about the situation from your spouse's point of view, even if you think he is wrong.** Remember, you need this person to sign your agreement. If you only think of your own perspective, you'll never get resolution.

- **Don't interpret what is going on based only on your fears.** Resist the urge to turn everything into a catastrophe. You will get through this.

- **Don't blame.** Blame doesn't get you anywhere, especially not now.

- **Let your spouse blow off steam and don't take it personally.** Not everything is an invitation to fight, and even if it is, you're not coming to that party.

- **Listen.** Acknowledge your spouse's feelings without being patronizing.

- **Be direct; don't play games.** Have your own priorities straight.

Though many of these points are common sense, when the relationship gets tangled up in the problem, things can get volatile fast—and common sense gets lost. When you are hard on people, they are no longer open and available to you to help with the problem. You end up with a problem *plus* an argument to solve. When your spouse knows he is safe from automatically being blamed for a situation, he'll be able to think strategically rather than defensively. You'll be able to work cooperatively and collaboratively rather than at odds with each other.

KEY 2. UNDERSTAND THAT ACKNOWLEDGING AND LISTENING ARE NOT THE SAME AS OBEYING

It may have been a long time since you've really listened to each other. When people argue, generally they're just waiting for their turn to talk—or simply talking over each other. They're not listening to what the other person is saying.

In order to settle your divorce and to redefine your relationship and family, you're going to need to listen to each other harder than ever. But listening is not the same thing as obeying. You don't have to do what your spouse wants just because she wants it. But people will not change their minds until they feel heard. Your job is to listen and understand your spouse's perspective.

By following these simple tips, you can unilaterally change the dynamic in your relationship and start on the path toward settlement and peace. Even if your spouse is being critical and demanding, you have the power to listen without getting defensive:

- Be still and quiet while you listen to your spouse, even if he seems very upset.

- Separate the words (the content) from the demanding tone.

- If it is appropriate, jot down a few notes about what your spouse is saying.

- Tell your spouse what you think you heard. Repeat it back in your own words as a summary.

- Tell your spouse you need time to think about it before you respond.

- Encourage your spouse to take time to think about requests that you make, too. She doesn't have to make up her mind right this minute.

- Realize that when your spouse is pressured to agree with you, agreements rarely stick. The only thing worse than getting divorced once is having to do the same divorce over again, so creating a lasting agreement is worth the effort.

It pays to listen hard. If you and your spouse have been tuning each other out in the months leading up to your divorce, each of you actively hearing what the other has to say can help rebuild some of the lost respect and trust. When people know you are listening, they don't have to scream anymore. When your spouse feels heard, he is less apt to have the need to hammer a point over and over. Conversations can move from mudslinging to creative problem solving more quickly.

KEY 3. USE "I" STATEMENTS

"I" statements are conflict resolution magic. The best part is that they're simple to incorporate into your habits. And, for the recipient, the "I" statement request is easier to honor. "I feel sentimental about keeping my grandmother's pots and pans" makes a much more peaceful case for keeping them than "You can't take all our kitchen stuff."

"I" statements create collaboration and build on personal responsibility rather than blame.

The opposite of the "I" statement is the "You" statement. "You" statements are inherently judgmental. They feel like an accusation (and usually are). A "You" statement is your opinion of the other person.

Imagine your spouse saying any of the following things to you:

- You are crazy.

- You can't do that.

- You are so lazy.

- You are loud.

- You are wrong.

An "I" statement gives your spouse information about you. It doesn't put your spouse on the defensive, because you are the vulnerable one. Imagine your spouse saying any of the following to you:

- I am feeling very insecure about having to support myself after so many years.

- I am so resentful of how much money we are spending on this divorce.

- I do not want to feel like I am not a part of my kids' day-to-day life.

- I am so angry that you introduced your girlfriend to the kids without letting me know first.

There is nothing to get defensive about when your spouse is merely telling you something about herself. You are not responsible for how she feels or to help her feel differently. This type of information sharing helps foster communication. It makes no judgments or demands.

To create an "I" statement, start your sentence with "I" and then use healthy personal disclosure to tell your spouse what is going on with you. Simply saying "I'd feel so much more financially secure if you could pay off your student loan" goes a lot further than "You racked up that debt, not me."

"I" statements are an easy way to show your spouse you are comfortable expressing vulnerability as you divorce. Since they are clearly your opinion or your feelings, and not a command for the other person, they are much easier for the other person to hear. They also verbalize a sense of yourself as separate from the "we" the two of you once were and allow you to take personal responsibility for your thoughts and feelings. Practice using them in all your relationships, not just with your spouse, so you can get used to thinking in terms of "I" statements all the time.

KEY 4. GIVE THE BENEFIT OF THE DOUBT

Before, during, and after your divorce, you're going to have lots of opportunities to test your ability to give your spouse the benefit of the doubt.

Here's an example: Your spouse is late for a meeting with the bank to see if you can refinance your house. Your first inclination is to take it personally. "How dare she be late again! She does this just to drive me crazy!" But there are also thousands of other plausible explanations which have nothing to do with you: the line at the grocery store was long, and the checker was new; the hamster got out of the cage and had to be found before leaving the house; an important phone call came from a family member at an inopportune time and she didn't have the heart to tell the caller to put a lid on it.

Maybe these explanations are true and maybe they aren't. If this is not habitual behavior, then find it within yourself to extend the benefit of the doubt. If it's just once in a while, it's ultimately easier on everyone not to take it personally. Your blood pressure will thank you.

Anytime you feel frustrated, annoyed, or mildly irritated, remember that your spouse is human and so are you. We all have our bad days. Also, one day you may be the one asking for the benefit of the doubt, and it helps to pay it forward.

Offering the benefit of the doubt helps you practice seeing the best in your spouse. Perhaps you haven't seen that in a while. Maybe that's because you've been looking for the worst. You and your spouse are both good people who are going through a very hard time right now. Allow your spouse to save face, and when it's your turn to ask for the same favor, it will be an easier request to honor.

KEY 5. HAVE AWKWARD CONVERSATIONS IN REAL TIME

Difficult conversations don't get easier with the passage of time. They get harder, and the difficulty is compounded if it looks like you tried to hide something or to be dishonest. When you need to have an awkward conversation, have it sooner rather than later. And if you can have it preemptively, it's even less awkward. Imagine your spouse telling you "I missed the mortgage payment that was due two weeks ago" instead of "I missed the mortgage payment that was due today" and better still "I think I am going to miss the mortgage payment that is due in two weeks. What do you think we should do?"

Before you have an awkward conversation, you can prepare yourself with the following exercise:

- Identify why you feel the conversation will be awkward.

- Is there anything you can do to make the situation better *before* you have to have the conversation? If so, do it.

- Have the conversation as soon as you're sure you need to have it, not at the last minute.

- Be honest. Sugarcoating the truth is just going to look deceitful at this point.

- What do you expect your spouse's reaction to be? Is there anything you can do or say to make that situation better?

- Make an appointment with your spouse to talk about the awkward situation, at a time and place where you can have a real conversation, out of earshot of the kids.

- Frame your conversation and acknowledge that it's awkward.

- Listen to your spouse's reaction and acknowledge that you're listening.

- Ask for help to problem solve.

For example: You are going to be late dropping off the children for the second time this week. You call your spouse forty-five minutes *before* you're supposed to drop the children off. "I am so sorry, but I can already tell I'm going to be late. I don't blame you for being upset with me. I am upset with me, too. Given the situation, should I just take them straight to the sitter? Or what would help you most? And sometime next week, can we talk about adjusting the drop-off time so this doesn't keep happening?"

Establishing a pattern of having awkward conversations right away, directly and honestly, can reduce a lot of unnecessary anxiety. If your spouse knows you're going to give him bad news as soon as you get it, he doesn't have to torture himself with his imagination. If he knows you want the same thing from him, he doesn't have to procrastinate about having those difficult conversations.

KEY 6. KEEP THE CONVERSATION GOING—
LIFE IS A DIALOGUE

The conversations associated with divorce can be tense and sad, but it is critical that you keep the dialogue going. One of the biggest mistakes you can make right now is to give your spouse the silent treatment or fail to keep trying to improve your relationship. You may need to take tiny steps in that direction and take a periodic time-out to clear your head. Even if you don't share children, it's still easier to have a decent relationship than a horrible relationship. When your friends are deciding which of you to invite to a party and realize they can invite both, or when you need to borrow your former spouse's truck, or when you run into your mother-out-law in the grocery store, you'll be rewarded for your efforts over and over again.

If you are tempted to shut down communication with your spouse, are you telling the truth, or are you stonewalling? When you are tempted to say any of the following, check in with yourself and make sure you aren't just making an excuse to avoid talking with your spouse:

- I just need some space right now.
- I want to give him the time he needs to think things through.
- I am sick of our fighting and needed a time-out.

- She pushed me away.

- He told me he wanted his privacy right now.

- I've been busy with my own life.

Sometimes *not talking* is the best option, especially if you feel like you're ready to blow a gasket. However, stonewalling tactics, like stalling, refusing to answer questions, hindering discussion, or bluntly refusing to cooperate with your spouse are forms of passive aggression, which are no more effective than screaming at each other. Stonewalling is destructive and punitive.

If you genuinely need a cooling-off period, ask for one. If you sense that your spouse needs a break, say, "I feel like we should take a few days to think about this, so I will be incommunicado until Thursday, and then I'll give you a call, okay?"

If your spouse shuts down dialogue with you, you will have to take responsibility and approach him. Here are some things you can do:

- **Use Key 4.** Don't take it personally and give your spouse the benefit of the doubt. Is he cutting off communication or taking the time he needs to cool off?

- **Use Key 5.** If you're avoiding a conversation because it will be difficult, find a way to have the conversation that's safe, with plenty of time to talk about a problem, including the right for either of you to say, "Let's end here for now and finish this discussion later," at any time, without a fight.

- **Don't get defensive.** Cut your spouse some slack. She may not have the same terrific communication skills that you have. Allow her some room to make the mistake of not having a new way to deal with an old hurt. Know that the only way to change the situation is to change the way you react to it.

- **Look within.** Is it possible that you could have hurt your spouse in some way or been insensitive? Maybe without even realizing it? Have you been upholding your end of the agreements so far in your divorce proceedings? If you don't know, ask. Open the door to conversation.

- **Prepare an icebreaker.** Think about what you want to say and what tone of voice you will use, and then practice it out loud so you can check yourself and modulate accordingly. You might try something like "Is everything okay? We haven't finished our conversation about the parenting plan yet and I am hoping you are ready."

- **Apologize even if you are unsure.** A simple "I am sorry if I have done something lately to hurt or offend you" will go a long way.

- **Be patient.** If your spouse tells you at this point that he is not ready to talk to you, suggest a cooling-off period and set a time to talk again soon (within a few days). If no time is a good time, or you can't talk without fighting, ask for help from a neutral source, like a therapist, member of the clergy, or mediator.

Keep the positive, respectful conversation going as much as possible. Most attempts to directly shut your spouse out are punitive and a way to mask your own hurt. Remember your divorce mission statement and align your behavior with the goals you set for yourself.

KEY 7. ASK YOURSELF "WOULD I RATHER BE HAPPY OR RIGHT?"

One of our most basic human longings is to be happy. Yet arguments make emotionally stable people unhappy.

If you'd rather be happy than right, consider these statements:

- Stop telling people how to do things, even simple things like which parking spot to take.

- If you hear someone make an error in simple conversation, don't correct them, especially if it is immaterial to the story.

- Let everyone be right. In each person's mind he or she is anyway.

- Take every opportunity to let go of being right, particularly if your being right means making others wrong.

- You can't expect everyone in the world to think the same way you do.

- Consider this: You can be right *for yourself* and also be happy, so you can have it both ways. The rub is you must also extend this liberty to everyone else, especially your spouse.

Being right doesn't automatically lead to happiness. People who are happy with themselves know what's right *for them* and trust everyone else to know the same. Use this time to help yourself and your spouse differentiate from each other. Your spouse's opinions aren't a reflection on you anymore, and vice versa. Give her latitude to form a new identity and recapture parts of herself she may feel she lost while you were married.

KEY 8. BE EASY TO TALK TO

If you fly off the handle every time your spouse comes to you with a problem, eventually he will stop coming to you. Even if you'd prefer not to hear bad news, it's generally better if you know. Make it easy for someone to tell you something that you don't want to hear: "Wow, that is really disappointing, but I'm really glad you told me. I really appreciate that you were straight with me."

Make it clear that you'd prefer to know before bad news happens: "If something happens with the kids and your new boyfriend, please tell me first so we don't put them in the middle. I promise that I won't be judgmental." At the same time, be willing to break bad news to your spouse: "I know you aren't going to want to hear this, and it's hard for me to bring it up, but I'd rather that you hear it from me, now, than from the neighbors."

Use your body language and facial expressions to show you are open, listening, and engaged. Listen actively and reframe what's been said: "Let me make sure I understand . . ." Make sure your spouse feels heard. Be on the same level as your spouse (sitting or standing). Be as gentle as you can at the start of a difficult conversation, no matter who brings it up.

Using the 8 Keys to Resolving Family Conflict

Using these 8 simple keys will revolutionize your divorce experience as well as your home life—and can even improve your life at work. They're easy to practice and implement once you get started.

In the next chapter, you will learn the 8 peace practices, which you can use to help you feel calmer on a daily basis. When tensions arise, you'll be operating from a more peaceful baseline and be more apt to remember to use the 8 keys to resolving family conflict. The 8 keys and the 8 peace practices *along with* your divorce mission statement give you the fundamental tools for peacemaking on which you'll build through the rest of the book—and the rest of your life.

CHAPTER 4

The 8 Peace Practices

> If you pump casually, you will pump forever. Pump hard to
> begin with and keep it up until you get that water flowing.
> Then a great deal will happen.
>
> —ZIG ZIGLAR

You will significantly enhance the peacemaking skills you acquired with the 8 keys to resolving family conflict by using the 8 peace practices contained in this chapter. As you do the 8 peace practices, you will create a personal reserve of sanity you can draw on when things aren't going your way. The practices will prepare you for the tense, disappointing, and sad moments in your divorce so you can move through them gracefully rather than merely coping.

We know it's overwhelming to add new activities to your life and to try to change your habits. The 8 peace practices are worth the investment of your time and attention because they will enhance your ability to think clearly and creatively. You will be the eye of the storm when settlement discussions get tense. You will project more poise with your spouse, children, coworkers, and friends.

And if it seems too difficult to implement both the 8 keys to resolving family conflict and the 8 peace practices, keep in mind that others (and especially your children) will experience your divorce based more on how the situation looks and feels to them than on what you say. If you explain to your children that Mom and Dad are divorcing so that the two of you can both be happy, but they see you frazzled, angry, and depressed, they won't believe you. Neither will anyone else. You run the risk of your children thinking the divorce is their fault, setting them up to be poorly adjusted afterward. Invest the energy it takes to change, because the payoff will be worth it.

The 8 Peace Practices

1. Breathing Exercise

2. Anchoring Technique

3. De-escalation Techniques

4. Self-Care

5. Challenging a Thought

6. Dismissing a Thought

7. 10-10-10 Rule

8. Your Divorce Story

1. BREATHING EXERCISE

Yes, we know you've heard it before, but breathing exercises are used to improve and bring calmness into many areas of life. They're used in weightlifting, stress management, martial arts, and childbirth, just to name a few. Steady, connected, abdominal breathing calms your mind, nerves, and emotions. It is a way to come down from high alert without getting an adrenaline hangover. Breathing deeply and mindfully creates a calming physical reaction. Don't believe us? Try it once.

The stress of your divorce puts your body into the state of high alert known as the fight-or-flight response. Even if you want to calm down, it can be difficult to do with so much adrenaline coursing through your bloodstream. Stress shuts down your critical thinking and leaves you with basically two solutions to every problem you face: run for the hills or all-out war. Neither of these is an option for you at this point. You must have settlement discussions with your spouse, and they will not be effective if you shut down or fight the entire time.

When people are nervous and upset, they typically hold their breath. Next time you're stressed out, notice whether you're holding your breath or breathing shallowly. You probably are. Simply reminding yourself to breathe when you're having a fight-or-flight moment is a victory.

We recommend that you do the breathing exercise twice a day, in the morning and the evening, and whenever you can fit it in. If you think you don't have time for it, consider that it takes about the same amount of time it does to drink a cup of coffee. It is totally passive and doesn't require any equipment besides a timer.

1. Find a quiet place where you won't be disturbed.

2. Sit comfortably wherever you want (a chair, the couch, the floor).

3. Make sure you are warm enough.

4. Set a timer for fifteen minutes (a kitchen timer, your cell phone).
   If you only have three minutes, do it for three minutes. This
   exercise is still worth doing even if you only have sixty seconds.

5. Close your eyes.

6. Breathe through your nose. If your nose is stuffed up, you
   can breathe through your mouth.

7. Breathe from your belly, not your shoulders.

8. Breathe naturally and audibly, but do not pause between
   breaths. As soon as you are done exhaling, begin inhaling.

9. Keep breathing continuously until your timer goes off letting you know that fifteen minutes have passed.

It doesn't matter what you think about during the breathing
exercise; it is not meditation. The goal is to defuse stress and leave
you oxygenated, calm, and assertive. The exercise will energize
you in the morning and relax you in the evening. You can also use
the breathing exercise anytime you're stressed out.

The breathing exercise will affect you immediately *and* it is also
cumulative. If you can't sit still for fifteen minutes the first time
you try it, do what you can and build up to fifteen minutes. If you
can't fit the exercise in twice a day in the beginning, do it once. If
you can't do it every day, do it three times a week. Above all, do
not beat yourself up for not being perfect or "doing it right." The
important thing is to keep trying. Once you notice the benefits of
the breathing exercise, you won't have to discipline yourself to do
it, because it will become second nature.

If you can only do one of the 8 peace practices for now, we recommend the breathing exercise. Once you begin to enjoy its benefits, you will have more time and energy for the other practices.

2. ANCHORING TECHNIQUE

The anchoring technique uses your mind's natural tendencies toward association to help you control your emotions. Anchoring happens naturally all the time. We feel a strong emotion and experience a smell or gesture at the same time. From then on, whenever that smell or gesture appears in our environment, we experience the same strong emotion. The smell of pumpkin pie may immediately transport you back to your family Thanksgiving celebrations when you felt safe and loved. The smell of bleach may remind you of the day you threw up at school in second grade and leave you anxious.

You can create anchors deliberately, using the following technique:

1. Choose the way you want to feel in a particular situation (for example, you want to feel confident and collected when you see your wife with her new boyfriend).

2. Recall a strong example of a time when you felt this way.

3. Close your eyes and take several deep breaths until you feel relaxed.

4. Use your memory of the past example to feel the emotion as strongly and vividly as possible.

5. When you are feeling the desired emotion quite intensely, create an anchor or physical association (for example, press your thumb and forefinger together, make a fist, touch your nose, or pull your earlobe).

6. Hold the gesture for a few seconds until the desired emotion fades.

7. Open your eyes.

After you have created your anchor, test it by making the gesture and seeing if it sets off the desired emotion. You can strengthen your anchor by repeating the technique several times in a row and using a different memory of the desired emotion each time.

Any time you are in a situation where you need to have the feeling you anchored, make the gesture associated with it. If you anchored in feeling peaceful by pressing your thumb and forefinger together, next time you feel tension rise between you and your spouse, press them together to elicit the feeling.

3. DE-ESCALATION TECHNIQUES

When emotions are running high, a fight with your spouse can erupt out of nowhere and take on a life of its own. Just because your spouse is getting amped up doesn't mean you have to match the level of aggression. You can de-escalate the intensity of the anger and bring the volatility to a level that will allow the two of you to process an issue or solve a problem.

Anger is like an onion. It has many layers. The top layer is the anger you're seeing: the angry words, gestures, and tone. But underneath is something more tender: fear, love, or sadness. So when

---

SHOUTING

While it's unpleasant to be on the receiving end of shouting, remember that the words hold clues to why your spouse is really upset. If you can get past the volume and tone, listen to the content in order to hear your spouse's concerns. Once you know the concerns, you can start to address them in the settlement, or at least work through the issues.

your spouse is angry, listen for what's underneath the words. "You are really trying to rip me off in this divorce" probably means "I'm scared that I won't be financially secure afterward." And "You're such a monster" probably means "I can't believe we've come to this. I thought we'd be in love forever."

Telling someone to "calm down" is probably the least effective way to get someone who's upset to calm down. In fact, saying anything judgmental or negative about your spouse's composure ("Don't you dare talk to me like that!") is definitely not a de-escalation technique. Neither is "I can see you are very upset, so let's come back to this when you can calm down."

Don't resist your spouse's yelling or she will crank it up that much higher to try to get through to you. Make intermittent eye contact because avoiding eye contact altogether will make your spouse think you are avoiding the situation, and he is likely to get even more confrontational. Conversely, keeping constant eye contact is a sign of aggression.

Detach yourself from the situation and watch your spouse get angry as though you were watching a movie. It may feel uncomfortable, but you wouldn't get up and yell at a movie screen. Simply observe.

When your spouse yells at you, most of what she says is likely exaggerated or simply not true. "You never paid attention to me" or "You always spent way too much money" is an irrational generalization. Nobody does something "never" or "always." And when you peel back the onion, the real hurt comes through. "You never paid attention to me" becomes "Am I that unlovable?" and "You always spent way too much money" becomes "I'm terrified that our money mismanagement is going to affect our financial security."

To de-escalate the situation, try any of the following techniques:

- **Listen.** Just sit and listen, allowing your spouse to vent. Sometimes that's all he needs. Let him go on with his diatribe and get it all out of his system. Let your spouse know you aren't going to attack back by saying "Okay. Go on." Nod your head in agreement. The goal in listening is to allow the anger to run its course and eventually sputter out. As you listen, be cautious not to appear patronizing or insincere since that will escalate the situation.

- **Agree.** Try to put yourself in your spouse's shoes and understand *why* she is angry. Calmly say, "I can see why you are so mad. That would make me mad, too." Even if you think that your behavior that prompted your spouse's anger was justified, you should try to understand and acknowledge why your spouse might have a different interpretation of the situation. You want to show your spouse that you know she has a right to express anger, and that you understand that there are different ways of looking at a problem. Most important, you need to get underneath the anger to deal with what is really going on.

- **Say, "I'm sorry."** You can say you are sorry without assuming all the blame for your spouse's anger. If your spouse is angry at you for something you did, apologize right away, even if you feel you have a legitimate excuse and didn't mean any harm. You can deal with the particulars once he calms down. Saying "I'm sorry your feelings were hurt when I didn't tell you I introduced my new boyfriend to the girls" is not an apology that will defuse an argument. Rather, saying "I'm sorry I introduced my new boyfriend to the girls without talking to you first; that was a mistake" clearly demonstrates your efforts at collaboration.

- **Invite criticism.** Say "Is there anything else? I really want to get to the bottom of this. What else have I done to upset you?"

Wring the complaint dry. Be respectful, not taunting. You really want to exhaust the list so that you can be done with this issue, hopefully forever. Chances are you did do something that your spouse took too personally, which caused her to get angry. It is a brave act on your part to invite criticism, and it will allow your spouse to get all the issues out in the open. They are bound to come out at some point anyway.

Both of you will have anger, disappointment, fear, and other strong emotions to deal with during this process. How well you and your children will adjust to your divorce is directly related to how well you and your spouse deal with these feelings. If you deal with anger using these techniques, over time your spouse's attacks and anger will either defuse and become less frequent, or they'll stop bothering you. Either way, you will unilaterally change the dynamic. And changing ugly dynamics is key to a divorce that successfully lets you move on into your new life.

4. SELF-CARE

We recommend that you deal with your divorce the same way you would deal with facing a serious health crisis. The stress of a divorce is similar in many ways. Nurturing and caring for yourself is an important way to soothe the pain associated with divorce and make better decisions. If you have been depressed or stressed during the time leading up to your divorce, you may have neglected yourself. You can turn this transition into a time of intense renewal as you redefine yourself. You don't need a complete makeover in just one day, but being aware that there are some mundane yet practical and effective things that you can do to take care of yourself, physically and emotionally, will bring you great benefits.

- **Exercise regularly.** Rather than focus on a cosmetic aspect of exercise like losing weight, focus on the stress-reduction benefits. Choose something that you know you can stick with, like walking. If you can, get outside in the fresh air. Leave your headphones at home once in a while so you can use the time to be alone and think. If you only have time for five minutes today, start with that—and tomorrow make it ten.

- **Resist the temptation to self-medicate.** Dealing with your pain by smoking, drinking, or doing recreational drugs can cloud your thinking and lead to addiction, so steer clear. Self-medicating only masks the problems rather than solving them; if you do become reliant on substances for self-soothing, you've just added to your problems rather than subtracting.

- **Get plenty of rest.** Worrying about your divorce may take a toll on your sleep schedule. Try to go to bed at the same time every night. Before you hit the sack, wind down with a warm bath, cup of tea, or another activity that calms you down. Avoid activities and substances that will disturb your sleep cycle. If you chronically need help sleeping, talk to your doctor.

- **Eat well.** Eat a good diet that works for you and your body type. Avoid mood swings that are caused by fluctuations in your blood glucose. Stay hydrated. Steer clear of foods that rob you of energy like sugary snacks and energy drinks.

- **Good grooming.** Don't neglect your hygiene. Take a shower and get dressed every day. Neglecting personal grooming can lead to depression. Besides, if you look your best, you will feel better about yourself, and others will respond accordingly.

- **H.A.L.T.** This is a slogan borrowed from recovery programs which stands for Hungry, Angry, Lonely, or Tired. It is important to stay in touch with your inner feelings and needs. Make sure you are not feeling hungry, angry, lonely, or tired before you have an important conversation regarding your divorce (or an important conversation about anything). Find appropriate ways to get these needs met.

5. CHALLENGING A THOUGHT

Most of us are hard on ourselves and very self-critical, especially when we're having a bad day. And you're going to have a lot of bad days when you're getting divorced. When we are in a bad mood, depressed, or stressed out, we may believe a thought that does not serve our best interests. The result can be a series of thoughts that produces a downward spiral of negativity that isn't even based in reality. Watch for this kind of negative thinking so you can challenge your self-criticism. Your third grade teacher called this "stinking thinking," and your teacher was right. If you would not say whatever it is that you're thinking about yourself to your best friend, don't say it to yourself. You deserve better, especially from yourself.

- **Black-and-white.** Don't let yourself engage in all-or-nothing thinking: "I am a total loser. I never finished my college degree because the plan was that my wife was the breadwinner and I'd stay home to work on my guitar music and raise the children. Now we are getting divorced and I can't find a job without a degree." No situation is that highly polarized. There are always gray areas. You may not have a bachelor's degree, but you have many other skills that will go largely ignored if you think you are a failure.

- **Exaggeration.** The stress of divorce can cause you to blow a negative event way out of proportion: "I have no idea how I am going to pay the mortgage without my husband's income. I am going to lose the house and end up living on the street, eating garbage from a Dumpster." Divorce is uncomfortable, sad, and awful, but it is not the end of the world—and you will survive. You have options about how to pay the mortgage, like getting a roommate or a second job. When you see anything in catastrophic terms, you shut down your ability to think creatively and problem solve.

- **Minimization.** Be careful not to let yourself become deflated with negativity after a very positive event occurs: "We sold the house the first week it was on the market and the buyers gave us $2,000 over the asking price because they love the swimming pool and wanted to move in before school starts. But all I can think of is how I'll never be able to find a house I will like as much as that one." Allow yourself to enjoy the little successes along the way in your divorce process. You loved this house, and you'll find another place to live that you love, too.

- **Ignoring the positive.** Don't let your grief cloud good things with negativity: "Since my separation, my girlfriend from high school, who is also single, called me several times to make sure I'm okay and invite me to dinner. But I know she is just doing that because she feels sorry for me." Give your friends and family the benefit of the doubt. Their concern is probably genuine because they care about you—and you have positive attributes, which you are ignoring.

- **Selective attention.** Be sure you look at the big picture so you aren't just seeing things that reinforce the negativity you feel. "I really got taken advantage of when we divided up the kitchen stuff. I wanted the mixer that matched my kitchen so bad, but my husband took it because it belonged to his mother." The person in this example is ignoring the fact that she got all the wedding china and flatware plus half of the appliances. Her entire focus is on what she did not get, selectively omitting the positive. The glass can be half-empty or half-full. Same glass.

6. DISMISSING A THOUGHT

When you notice you are thinking in a way that doesn't serve your best interests, you can dismiss it. Think of your mind as a garden and negative thoughts as weeds. If you pull them up as soon as you see them, they won't grow so big that they take over the positive thoughts that you'd prefer to have flower there. This will take practice. You will make mistakes. The more you do it, though, the better you will get at recognizing these destructive and negative thoughts early on.

- **Is it true?** Simply asking yourself if a negative thought you are having is true is one way to drop the thought. "I can't believe I am getting divorced. I am such an awful person." Is that true? Are you really a horrible person? Do you really have no redeeming qualities whatsoever? Of course not. And if you have done some things you're not proud of, maybe this is the wake-up call you needed. Maybe you can't make amends that will change the fact that you're getting divorced, but you can change how you behave going forward in your divorce, in your next relationship, and every day.

- **Erase the thought.** When a negative thought enters your mind, see it written out on a whiteboard and then imagine erasing it. If it is particularly persistent, write the thought on a piece of paper and tear it up.

- **Cancel.** If you say something negative out loud, immediately say to yourself, "Cancel," and replace it with a positive thought. "Being single is horrible. Oops. Cancel! I mean, I'll have to adjust to being on my own and I look forward to meeting new people."

- **Change the dial.** Imagine you have a remote control for the various thought channels available to you, and if you don't like what's going on in your head, change the channel.

- **What did you learn?** Some of our most negative thinking has to do with regret. What did you learn from the situation about which you are thinking negatively? "If only I hadn't been so focused on my career, then I wouldn't have lost Ethan to another woman." You may not be able to repair your marriage and stay with your current spouse, but at least you have learned something you can take into your next relationship.

7. 10-10-10 RULE

Inspired and adapted from Suzy Welch's *10-10-10: A Life-Transforming Idea*, this very simple concept to help you evaluate your choices is based on both the present and future impact they'll have. When you feel the compulsion to do or say something and are not sure whether you should, consider the following:

- How will I feel about this in 10 minutes?

- How will I feel about this in 10 months?

- How will I feel about this in 10 years?

Say you arrive at your spouse's house to pick up some of your personal belongings that she has agreed to box up for you. She said she would take care of it because it would upset her too much to watch you do it. Typically, she is immaculate. However, this time, your stuff has been shoved into garbage bags. You want to yell at her, "What is wrong with you? You *said* you were going to box this stuff up! Had I known you were going to treat my things like *garbage* I would have never agreed to let you touch it!"

Ask yourself:

- How will I feel about this in 10 minutes? (Pretty good! I can't believe she snowed me into thinking she was going to take care of my wardrobe when she held it over my head in our marriage. She deserves to be yelled at.)

- How will I feel about this in 10 months? (Embarrassed. She was upset. Part of the reason we divorced was because I travel so much for work and I understand now it was probably therapeutic for her to cram my clothes in a garbage bag. I shouldn't have yelled at her. I should have asked her what was wrong that made her do that.)

- How will you feel about this in 10 years? (Like a total idiot. Who yells at someone over a bag of suits? So it cost me $100 to get them cleaned again. They needed it anyway. I hope the kids forgot all about it.)

Remember that many times during your divorce trivial things may set you off. When you feel a high negative charge, there is something else going on. The 10-10-10 Rule will help you stick to your mission statement as you consider the short- and long-term consequences of your actions. Negativity is like the junk food of emotions. It tastes good while you are eating it, but months and years later you're still trying to undo the damage.

8. YOUR DIVORCE STORY

You are creating a story about your divorce that is based on the reality of your decision to divorce and the divorce proceedings as well as your thoughts and feelings about what is going on in your life as you divorce. Your divorce story is what you hear yourself saying in your head about what is going on. It is also what you hear yourself telling others. Ideally, it also creates your own optimistic way of looking at your situation. If your divorce story is negative, you have the power to rewrite it.

If you perceive yourself as a victim, your story will be based largely on how horrible your spouse is and how your spouse ruined your life. If you perceive yourself as a hero, your story will be about how you are making the best of your divorce and trying to move on in a respectful way.

The way you think and talk about your divorce will strongly influence how you act and the decisions you make. A negative story will insure that your past poisons your future. If you find yourself obsessively telling your horror story, you have entered the toxic zone. You can become so trapped in your negative divorce story that it becomes more compelling than anything good that is going on in your life right now. Your story will seem more true every time you tell it, so it is up to you to author a story that leaves you open to let go of your grievances and move on.

The tenor of your divorce story will depend on your ability to deal with your disappointment over getting divorced. As painful as it is, you must confront the reality of things not turning out the way you hoped without becoming jaded and bitter.

June's Divorce Story

June and Rich divorced after three years of marriage. They have a son, Henry. June used the prompts in the next section of this chapter to write up her divorce story. Allowing yourself the luxury of really thinking through the entirety of your marriage from beginning to end can be very cathartic. June wrote her divorce story in her notebook as follows:

> My husband Rich and I met when I was 29 and he was 32. A mutual friend introduced us. We were engaged after one year of dating and married six months after our engagement. My memories about our wedding day are mostly positive. I was really excited at the time. All our friends were there and it was a lovely event.
>
> We were really in love in the beginning and I am grateful we were married. Rich was very supportive of me while I was starting my career. Most of all I am grateful for our son Henry. Rich is a terrific father.
>
> We decided to divorce after 3 years of marriage and to have a peaceful divorce. We really wanted to mediate. I felt bad enough for wanting to leave. The last thing I wanted to do was create more heartache than we were already experiencing.
>
> When people ask me why we got divorced, I tell them because we no longer wanted to be married and leave it at that. I am so sad that this is happening, but I also know that it's the right thing to do and I'm mostly confident that I can move on. I really want to.
>
> I really want Henry to have a better example of love to follow than what Rich and I could have shown him. We didn't fight a lot, but we stopped loving each other. How can that be good for Henry? I look forward to decorating my own home

and enjoying living independently. When Rich has Henry, I plan on using that time to teach piano lessons.

I hope that Rich finds someone who understands him more than I could and that he feels comfortable co-parenting with me. I also hope he prospers financially. He is a good man; we are just so different.

The thoughts I have about my divorce are mostly positive but I am still feeling some guilt that shows up in the way I tell my story to others. Sometimes I feel like I have to hide the fact that I am excited to be on my own because I don't want people to think I took the decision lightly or am selfish in leaving. I know other people may have stayed in a marriage that was unsatisfying but I just can't live that way. I need more passion.

My former in-laws are very disappointed. They are cold toward me now. My mother-in-law pulled me aside and told me that in her day, women kept their promises and that she'd had a bad feeling about me during my bridal showers. I want to improve things with them so for now I let them have their opinions about our divorce without defending our choice. I think it's best to give them the space they need to adjust. I can also encourage Henry to have an active relationship with his grandparents.

Some people who were Rich's friends before we got married seem to be holding grudges toward me but I can let go of the people I met through him and make new friends. Our mutual friends seem okay even though it is a little awkward. I've promised myself I'll never gossip or complain about Rich to them. Some of our friends have divorced, too.

When I notice myself thinking or talking negatively about my divorce or Rich, I'll get out my notebook and read my divorce mission statement. Golf is a good way to lift my spirits and exercise defuses my frustration. I've been doing the breathing exercise and it really soothes me.

My friends support me, too. I've already asked them to stop me if I start grousing to them about my divorce. I'll just tell them the positive things. Most of all, I need to show people I am happy with my decision through my actions. I have some divorced friends who came through it well and I can ask them how they did it.

Your Divorce Story

The two things that affect your divorce story most are your attitude and the amount of personal responsibility you are able to take. You can change your attitude any time you want to. You can stop blaming others for what "happened to you."

The idea is to write up a realistic view of your situation with a happy ending in mind. How can you frame your disappointment in ways that will help you accept it and let go?

Now it's time to write up your own divorce story in your notebook. Take some time alone when you won't be interrupted. Begin by doing the breathing exercise for fifteen minutes or as long as you feel comfortable. Re-read your divorce mission statement and then use the following prompts to suggest what you could include, along with whatever else you feel inspired to write about. You can rewrite your divorce story periodically through your divorce to reflect the new, positive changes that come into your life as you embrace the future and extend your optimism at each step of the process.

ELEMENTS OF YOUR DIVORCE STORY

My spouse's name

Age we each were when we met

Where/how we met

Engaged after how long dating?

Married after how long engaged?

My memories about our wedding day are (mostly positive or negative)?

We decided to divorce after (how many) years of marriage?

We decided to have a peaceful divorce because . . .

Some positive things I remember about the first year of our marriage are . . .

Some reasons I am grateful we were married are . . .

When people ask me why I got divorced, I tell them . . .

The feelings I have about my divorce are . . .

Some dreams of happiness I have for my newly single life are . . .

Some hopes of happiness I have for my spouse in (his/her) newly single life are . . .

The thoughts I have about my divorce are (mostly positive or negative)?

When I talk about my divorce, the tenor of my story is (mostly positive or negative)?

My relationship with my former in-laws is (mostly positive or negative)?

Some things I can do to maintain or improve my relationship with my in-laws are . . .

My relationships with mutual friends of my spouse's and mine are (mostly positive or negative)?

Some things I can do to maintain or improve the relationships with our mutual friends are . . .

When I notice my inner script of my divorce story is becoming negative, I will . . .

Support I will seek from friends and family to help me keep my divorce story positive includes . . .

Using the 8 Peace Practices

Use the peace practices that appeal to you whenever you have a chance. Though they are simple, the subtle shifts they create in the way you view your divorce and life after will keep you on your trajectory toward peace. The more you practice, the easier it gets. Remember that the breathing exercise is the backbone of the practices and try to fit it in every day. Go easy on yourself and everyone else. Try your best every day and know that some days you won't feel like trying at all, and that's okay.

CHAPTER 5

Set Your Emotional GPS to Goodness

Before you embark on a journey of revenge, dig two graves.

—CONFUCIUS

Many people claim it takes years to get over a divorce. It doesn't have to be that way. You don't have to hit rock bottom before you start to recover. If you let yourself (and your spouse) off the hook by letting go of blame, shame, and other unproductive emotions, you can make your divorce work. You can experience your grief and healing *as part of your divorce itself* and begin your new life right now.

The current divorce legal system encourages bad behavior, costs you money, and wreaks emotional havoc on your family. The court system wasn't set up to do that, but that's been the unintended outcome. During a divorce it is important to conserve your financial and emotional resources and acknowledge that an all-out divorce war could leave you too broken and financially devastated to move on. But you can move on from this marriage, learn from your mistakes, and serve as a role model for your children, your friends, and your community.

Whatever it was that made your marriage unsustainable doesn't have to predict whether and how you settle your divorce issues and successfully redefine your relationship with your former spouse. You can use the 8 keys to resolving family conflict and your favorite of the 8 peace practices to unilaterally change the way you and your spouse interact as you work through your divorce.

When you get caught up in the blame, shame, and shoulda-woulda-coulda, you miss opportunities to create forward-thinking solutions. Drama and havoc wreaking aren't necessary components of uncoupling. They're *typical* components of a divorce, but they aren't *necessary*.

In spite of any anger, fear, grief, and guilt you may feel around your divorce, you want to do the right thing by everyone concerned. Hold on to that thought throughout this process. Your behavior during your divorce won't always be perfect, but if you keep trying, you'll find your way.

Let the painful experiences in your life show you what you *don't* want. As long as you learn something from your marriage and divorce, neither was a mistake. You can't change the past, but you do have some control over the outcome. However, the most important thing *right now* is that you stop the hurting. You and your spouse don't have to vilify each other to justify your divorce. You can use your divorce to end your pain, not cause more.

Setting Your Emotional GPS

When you set your car's GPS for an address, that is where your path will take you. The same is true of your own emotional GPS. When you program your destination for goodness, that's where you'll end up.

There will be obstacles in your path, to be sure. And at times you may need to double back and start over. But when you use your good intentions and good faith efforts as your beacon, you will finish your divorce as you intended—happy, healthy, and whole.

The magic lies in your *intention to have a peaceful divorce.* You don't have to be a saint or a mystic to find peace. All you really have to do is decide to put an end to the conflict in your life and then keep moving in that direction. We call this setting your emotional GPS to goodness, embarking on a journey with peace as your destination. This chapter will show you how to do that.

To set your emotional GPS to goodness you will:

- **Forget perfect.** Making your divorce work isn't about being perfect. It's about participating fully in the process and not letting little mistakes you make along the way derail you. So you lost your temper and yelled at your spouse. Don't get discouraged; just try harder next time to keep your anger in check.

- **Forgive shortcomings.** You will learn more about this in chapter 9, "Forgiveness and Acceptance." Remember you're not expecting either of you to be perfect. Just do your best every day knowing that your best will be different depending on your mood, stress level, and many other factors.

- **Be nice.** Choose now to cause less pain in your life and in your spouse's life. We all behave badly from time to time and have been mean and vindictive on purpose. It's natural sometimes to want to make someone who's hurt you feel your pain. Resist that urge. It will do nothing to help make your divorce work.

- **Love the sinner but hate the sin.** Separate your bad behavior from who you are as a person. Don't obscure the way to peace by confusing a few low moments when you behaved badly with who you and your spouse really are.

- **Take responsibility.** Know the difference between what you can change and what you can't. When it comes to people, you can only change yourself. You are only in charge of your own emotional GPS and your own direction, so don't expect to dictate to your spouse which path to take.

- **Take the high road.** In each step of your divorce, ask yourself "What action can I take that will least likely end in regret?" and "If I do or say this, how will it help me with my goal of a peaceful divorce?"

- **Get better through practice.** Be determined to come out of your marriage better than you were going in.

Remember your real goal in life is to love, be loved, and have a good life. At the end of the day, this is all most of us really want.

Obstacles to Peace

Cultivating peace in your life is an ongoing process that requires constant vigilance. Along the way there will be countless obstacles that will throw you off course, which is why setting your emotional GPS is so important. Your journey will be that much longer and more difficult if you don't learn to accept imperfection and failure in yourself and your spouse, to handle the pain, to deal with conflict and criticism, and to let go of self-destructive habits.

How do you correct your course? What can you do to help yourself and your spouse keep moving toward your destination?

How do you orchestrate peace talks rather than fighting? How can you move beyond argument to dialogue?

The next sections describe roadblocks that may require you to recalculate, along with some ways to plow through or around them and get back on track. Common obstacles are:

- Expecting perfection—now
- Not dealing with pain
- Being critical
- Being defensive
- Being involved in your spouse's business
- Arguing and fighting

EXPECTING PERFECTION—NOW

Expecting everything to be perfect in your life now, especially when your entire sense of self is changing, can pile on the stress. It is unrealistic to expect that all the goals you have for your divorce and life after will be accomplished immediately. It took you months or years to get to this point, so it's unrealistic to expect your problems to be solved overnight. It will take time to solve things and readjust. You may need a couple of chances to get things right.

Perfectionism will lead you to being critical of yourself, your spouse, and your divorce process. It's wonderful to aim high and go for what you really want. This attitude will propel you toward your goals and help you take steps toward achievement. But expecting perfection is very draining because your impetus will be fear. Divorce is a journey, both during and after, not just a destination. Being too impatient is counterproductive.

Needing to have everything exactly as you want it to be can lead to disappointment in your progress. Maybe you haven't accomplished your top priority yet, but don't get bogged down in that. Surprisingly, these expectations can also cause you to procrastinate. If you are so worried that something won't go your way, you may not act in your own best interests, spinning a cycle of failure and more disappointment. Perfectionism can also lead to you being defensive or argumentative with your spouse if your ideas about what's "right" don't coincide when she gives her input about how she wants things to be.

If you expect perfection now, you may become overly critical toward yourself and become so set in thinking only about what your needs, wants, and wishes are that your all-or-nothing attitude leads to isolation. A constant critical eye turned toward the other people involved in your negotiations may push them away.

Overcoming Perfectionism

Here are some tips for overcoming your expectation that everything be perfect now:

- **Increase your tolerance for failure.** Wholesome discipline is wonderful. Beyond that, try to soften your taskmaster attitude. When you are feeling like you (or someone or something else) failed, jot your thoughts down in your notebook. Just because you lost it and argued one time doesn't mean you need to regress to all your past bad behaviors. Just vow to do it differently next time. Using your notebook will allow you to observe any tendency to be intolerant of situations and people that may not even be within your control. Simply observing how often you think things aren't good enough may help you see how being more tolerant can free you from unnecessary grief. By using your notebook on an ongoing basis, you'll also be able to see your progress.

- **One step at a time.** You won't reach any goal by demanding that you succeed immediately. Change takes time. The truth is you can't have everything you want right now, and when you get closer to your goal, it probably won't be perfect any-way. Do what you can for today and take each day one at a time. If you are having an especially bad day, take it one hour at a time. Rushing may cause you to miss something really important. Progress is your goal, not perfection.

- **Journey vs. destination mentality.** Celebrate the small vic-tories and take breaks along the way. Record your little tri-umphs in your notebook, and when you feel like you aren't getting anywhere, look back to see how far you've really come and take pride in your progress.

NOT DEALING WITH PAIN

As you orient your life away from negativity and toward peace, your fear, anger, and grief may sometimes draw you back into the patterns of hurt you developed as your marriage deteriorated. Feel-ing hurt over your divorce is normal, natural, and part of your healing. It can be so immense sometimes that it interferes with your daily routine. You may feel like you hurt too much to experi-ence any joy at all. When you have a headache, you can take a pain reliever. Not so with emotional pain.

Now is the time to trust your natural healing ability. A physi-cian can set a broken bone, but it is your body that does the actual healing. In the same way, cultivating your peacemaking skills will set the trajectory of your divorce toward peace, and alleviate your heartache.

Overcoming Emotional Pain

The way out of painful emotions is through them. On days when you feel particularly bad, keep the following in mind:

- Pain takes up a lot of energy and attention. It can provoke you into making impulsive moves. Be aware that while you are in pain you are vulnerable to making bad decisions, so take your time.

- You can cope! The less anxiety you have, the more clarity you will have. Use whichever of the 8 keys to resolving family conflict and the 8 peace practices work best for you to lower your anxiety and create a more peaceful baseline.

- Underneath your fear, anger, and grief is hidden wisdom for you to discover.

- Your intention to have a peaceful divorce and your natural yearning to be happy, healthy, and whole will give you the courage necessary to move through your pain.

- You can use your pain to cultivate a redefined relationship with your spouse based on giving each other a fresh start.

BEING CRITICAL

If you want to make your divorce work, be careful that you are not being critical of your spouse. It is normal and natural to have complaints to air with your spouse. However, if you are too hard on your spouse by criticizing, insulting, or personally attacking her as you discuss the problem, you'll never solve it.

Your spouse probably won't take your criticism well even if you feel like you are solving a problem or furthering a discussion. It feels hurtful and mean on the receiving end. It's hard to admit, but is your criticism actually meant to vent, be purposely hurtful, or make you feel superior?

Overcoming the Urge to Criticize

When you feel like there is something you absolutely must tell your spouse that you feel he might take as criticism, consider the following:

- **Check your motivation.** Are you trying to improve a facet of the way you two interact and promote positive change, or are you simply complaining? If you feel a strong emotional charge about what you want to say, make sure you're not just acting out your own frustration.

- **Suggest rather than criticize.** A positive suggestion is received far better than a criticism, and your spouse may even appreciate what you offer. Saying "I'd love it if you could help the kids stay organized by using this really cool online calendar I found" will come off better than "You are so unorganized."

- **Be clear about what you'd like to see.** Be as specific as possible. Rather than "I wish you wouldn't let the house get so messy when we're trying to sell it," try "Have you considered what a messy house looks like to a prospective buyer? Let's make a checklist of what needs to be done to keep the house show-ready so we can really get our money's worth."

BEING DEFENSIVE

As you set your emotional GPS to goodness, watch for any temptation to be defensive. Being defensive puts you automatically in victim mode instead of in charge of your future. Defensive attitudes, posturing, and comebacks escalate conflict. No matter how you express it, defensiveness is a way to protect yourself, which means you fear attack. Assuming attack is coming, you'll interpret even innocent comments through this filter, putting you at risk for conflict.

Overcoming Defensiveness

If you notice yourself becoming defensive, here are some things you can do:

- **Listen for information.** Hear the words as information, not as an attack. What is your spouse trying to communicate to you? Try to see things from her point of view and get to the core of the issue rather than assuming she is simply trying to hurt you. Remember that listening and acknowledging are not the same as obeying.

- **Don't take it personally.** Some of the difficult discussions are just that—difficult discussions. It's not all about you. You are not your divorce or any of the problems associated with it. Don't assume every criticism is meant as a slight to you. Be easy to talk to.

- **Don't always contradict.** Continually challenging what your spouse is trying to tell you with worlds like "Yes, but . . . ," "No," and "Well, you always . . ." shuts down communication. It is very important to keep the conversation going, so use words like "I see," "I'm listening," and "Tell me more."

BEING INVOLVED IN YOUR SPOUSE'S BUSINESS

It's a huge adjustment to go from being involved in every aspect of your spouse's life to leading separate lives. One of the ways you can get off course toward making your divorce work is by continuing to be involved in your spouse's business. By that we mean aspects of the way he is living his new life that as a *former* spouse you no longer have a say in.

Keep your involvement to the least you need to know and stop there. If you have children, there are things you'll need to know, like whether your spouse has their sports equipment, books, toys, or school papers. But you don't need to know how your spouse plans to spend Sunday afternoon, what she has in her refrigerator, or how her relationship with her sister is going. If you don't have children, you will need to know even less about what is going on in your spouse's new life. Stay out of your spouse's business as much as you possibly can. You need all your energy to run your own life.

Wishing your spouse would change is a waste of your time. You will likely find yourself embroiled in conflict any time you have a thought process that goes like this:

- My spouse is wrong about _____ and needs to change.

- I cannot be happy because he won't change.

Chances are the things you want to change about him now are the same things you wanted to change about him when you were married. He didn't change then and he's not going to change now. In fact, it may even seem worse because the little compromises you used to make for each other for the sake of the relationship are certainly not going to happen now that you are getting a divorce. Anticipate that.

If you need to be in your spouse's business in order to navigate your day-to-day relationship, keep it on a need-to-know basis. If your wife has a new boyfriend who has met your children, find out his name and a little bit about him so you can help normalize the situation with your kids. "I'm glad you had fun with Mommy and John at the state fair last weekend. That's terrific that you got to see the hogs" helps everyone feel comfortable. You don't want your kids to have secrets or taboo topics. On the other hand, you don't need to know "Is John as handsome as Daddy?" or "Did Mommy kiss him?"

You can't change your spouse or the way she is living her life, and it is inappropriate for you to even want to. If you pin your happiness on changing her, you are in for a lot of pain and disappointment. If you find yourself tempted to horn in on her life, focus on something you need to do for yourself. And never use your children as spies for you to find out what is going on in the other household, no matter how tempting it is. Now is the time to focus on your own life and happiness.

Overcoming Being Involved in Your Spouse's Business

The best way to stop being involved in your spouse's business and to focus on your own life is to let go. Letting go is not a passive surrender. Letting go is an active demonstration that you trust yourself to make the right decisions about your divorce. The ideas you are learning in this book will work for you if you allow them to.

Letting go means opening your mind to new insights. These insights will give you greater clarity to work with your spouse to create a win-win settlement and design your new life.

Letting go is relieving yourself—and your spouse—of guilt. You are not a horrible person or a failure for getting divorced, and neither is your spouse. You do not have to spend time and energy now justifying why you are getting divorced, since you have already made that decision. What matters is what you do with the situation.

Letting go is asking the question "Given where I am right now, what action can I take that will move me even one tiny step closer to wholeness, happiness, and health?" As long as you keep moving in that direction, you will get there, setbacks and all.

Letting go allows you to accept that there are some things you can't change and some things you can. For example, if you're struggling with what to do with a too expensive house, *you can't change* the fact that neither you nor your spouse will likely be able to afford the house on your own. *You can change* your focus to what you can do—like making minor repairs and cleaning the house so it will sell quickly and for a fair asking price. If you're struggling with how you behaved toward your spouse's family and the toll it took on your marriage, *you can't change* the fact that you weren't nicer to them. *You can change* by being nicer to your spouse's family during and after your divorce.

THE THINGS I CANNOT CHANGE

In your notebook, list people, issues, and circumstances that bother you, but that you know you cannot change. For each item, also note where you might be able to shift your focus toward personal responsibility and effect change where you can:

My spouse's parents blame me for our divorce and confront me with their anger every time I see them.

I cannot change this because: Their feelings are theirs and they are entitled to them.

Instead I will focus on: How I can manage my anger when they confront me so I don't allow myself to be drawn into the argument.

If you think through the things you cannot change, you can redirect your energy so you don't become frustrated and waste your time needlessly suffering about things over which you have no control. Focusing on what you *can change* puts you in charge of how you feel and provides insight into how you can make things better.

ARGUING AND FIGHTING

Be aware of any temptation to engage in conflict. Some arguments can be productive. However, arguing for the sake of the conflict itself isn't healthy, and it will throw you off course.

Conflict may be attractive for many reasons. Some people have experienced conflict in their home lives and marriages for so long that it feels normal. For others, it's a way of staying in touch; "conflict is contact" and is better than having no relationship at all.

It can also be very addictive. Some people just don't feel alive unless they are embroiled in something juicy, and others are afraid of what will happen if they stop defending themselves. Conflict also provides a means of procrastination, a distraction from having

HOW THEY STOPPED THE FIGHT

Karen and Jeff were married seven years and had two children. After their divorce, Karen agreed to help Jeff move into an apartment. They were working in a steady rhythm unloading the moving van and had agreed to put the boxes in the rooms as they were labeled (kitchen, bedroom, bathroom, etc.).

Karen was walking out to get another box from the van when Jeff said to her, "Do you mind handing me that box of kitchen stuff?" Annoyed, Karen said, "What do you mean hand you that box? Go over and get it yourself!" Jeff countered, "That's so ridiculous, I can't believe you won't just hand me that box."

Karen suddenly realized that if she countered again, they were going to start a fight over a box of kitchen utensils and scare the children, yet again. She stopped and said, "I'm sorry, that was really silly, of course I can hand you that box."

Jeff smiled, relieved, and they continued to unpack.

to think about what's next in your life. As long as there's drama, you don't have to think about settling your divorce, going back to school, getting a job, or whatever else you don't want to face. For some people, conflict feels safer than change.

It takes two people to fight. One of you is instigating and the other is acting out. There is not one perpetrator and one victim. You can refuse to be either.

If you find that you are fighting with your spouse out of an attraction to conflict rather than an attempt to problem solve, stop the argument and get back on track. The rest of this chapter deals with ways you can stop unproductive fighting throughout your divorce and after.

The surest way to shift the dynamic between you and your spouse is to simply stop fighting. Be clear that you aren't going to engage. Calmly state in an assertive tone "I am not going to fight with you about that." Your spouse may try to tempt you into participating and even resort to saying some very ugly things to get you to fight back. Eventually, if you are not taking the bait, your spouse will stop. This will take practice, but as you refuse to engage, you'll watch the anger defuse and eventually the provocations will stop, too.

Identify the fights you have over and over again, and ask your spouse to agree not to have those unproductive fights anymore. When they come up, you can say "We agreed we are not going to have that same fight again. If you need to say more on that topic, go ahead and I'll listen, but I am done fighting with you on that issue."

You can let an old conflict express itself without either of you being mean and without sniping at each other. If your spouse yells, attempting to engage you in a fight, listen to the words but don't get sucked in by the tone. This fight is information. You have hit on something that is important to him. Help your spouse release these old fights as you remember that he may fear that in letting go of the old argument, he is also letting go of a familiar part of his relationship with you.

When you suddenly refuse to fight, especially in the middle of an argument, be prepared for your spouse to be thrown off guard. One or both of you may even start laughing. That's when you'll know you've really made some headway!

Breaking Down a Fight

Underneath every dispute is an underlying issue to be solved. The fight is merely an expression of the strong feelings of anger, hurt, betrayal, abandonment, rejection, or other unarticulated emotion surrounding the issue. The key to breaking down a fight is for you and your spouse to allow each other to express the emotion and

ARE YOU GETTING WHAT YOU GAVE?

Is your request received with the same tone as it was given? If not, you've hit a hot button. Rather than react to the content, you can reframe the issue:

Request: I am concerned that the mortgage was late last month. This month can you make your part of the deposit on the twenty-ninth instead of the first?

Response: You're always so bossy! I don't have to do what you say anymore!

Reframe: You're right, you don't have to do what I say. But I know that your credit is important to you, so do you have another suggestion about how we can better coordinate the mortgage payment?

try your best to use *the information* to get to the root of the problem rather than continue with the same unproductive fight over and over.

Wait for a peaceful time when the fight is over and you can examine what happened separate from the negative emotion involved. Most disputes stem from things that happened in the past or an ongoing value conflict that has never been resolved. The first part of breaking down a fight is to look at what happened in the past that is still bothering you.

The second part of breaking down a fight is identifying why it is still bothering you. What is going on right now with the issue that you need to attend to? Why is something that happened in the past still occupying your time today?

The third part of breaking down a fight is identifying the pay-offs and costs associated with it. How does hanging onto this fight benefit you and work to your advantage? What does it cost you?

The fourth part of breaking down a fight is making a plan of action for how you can settle the dispute. What can you do right now to wrap up what happened in the past and move on? Is there anything you can take responsibility for and remedy? Do you owe someone an apology? Can you let go of the need for an apology you have been waiting for from your spouse?

Breaking Down a Fight: Brenda's Story

Brenda was married to Dean, her high school sweetheart, for twenty-one years. They had problems conceiving a child and, when they turned thirty, decided they would never have children and were both fine with that. When Brenda was thirty-nine, she found herself deeply dissatisfied in her marriage and asked Dean for a divorce. This came as no surprise to Dean because he and Brenda fought like cats and dogs. Neither of them could stand living in a perpetual war zone, but neither had had the courage to throw in the towel on their first and only relationship. The prospect of moving on was sad and terrifying, even though contempt had poisoned their marriage and there was no coming back from that.

Now that they were divorcing, Brenda was determined to get a handle on the fighting. She was exhausted from the negativity. Brenda thought about the prompts in the section that follows and was able to name the main fight she had with Dean and break it down into small parts so she could resolve it once and for all. The following is an entry from her notebook.

> The main fight I have with Dean is "I am not your mother." This fight usually starts when our house gets messy and I am feeling pressured to do something other than clean it up.
>
> When this fight is brewing between Dean and me, I am furious and resentful. I say things to him like "I can't believe you expect me to do your dishes for you. I'm not your mother and I can't believe you are not grown-up enough to take care of yourself."
>
> At the time I say those mean things to Dean, I really mean them. I have a lot of resentment toward him for expecting me to be a full-time housewife and work. Behind my anger I feel like Dean marginalizes me and doesn't appreciate me. I'm not sure he ever did. I do feel bad after being so mean to him but at the time it feels wonderful. I want him to hurt as much as I do.
>
> The fight usually ends with him squealing his tires and leaving. It's really awful. We have this fight at least once a week. It's like I can't stop picking at him.
>
> The benefit of staying in this dispute is that I can feel right and superior to Dean. It makes it easier to leave him if I call him a baby. The cost of staying in this dispute is that things have gotten really ugly between us and that makes me so sad.

What I really need from Dean is for him to tell me that it's okay for me to move on. I'm not sure he has that in him right now and he might not ever. Along with being hard, our divorce is embarrassing.

The one thing I can do to remove some of the tension from this fight is to stop picking up after him and let him keep his belongings any way he wants to. After all, we are divorcing. I can stand the mess for as long as it takes for one of us to move out.

Brenda decided to move her personal belongings into the basement and ignore Dean's stuff to save her sanity until they could separate. Their fighting dissipated and living on separate floors gave them the space they each needed to gain some perspective about transitioning out of their marriage after so long together.

Breaking Down a Fight: Your Story

Do you and your spouse have a fight that gets reignited over and over again? Wouldn't it be a relief to know that you never have to have that fight again if you don't want to? Even if you don't have one particular fight, being able to identify your conflict patterns is important.

Use the prompts below to break your fight down by writing about it in your notebook. As you think about the questions, the value to hold in mind is that you are trying to find a way to open the door in your dispute just a crack without compromising on what's most important to you. How can you do this? Write your ideas up in your notebook the way Brenda did. Be as detailed as you want to be. Fill in what you can now, and if you need to come back to it, you can.

Name your fight.

How does the fight usually start?

What are the negative feelings you express when this fight flares up?

What mean things do you say to your spouse that you end up regretting later?

What do you think is really behind the mean things you say to your spouse?

How does the fight usually end?

How often do you have this fight?

What are the benefits or payoffs to staying in this dispute?

What are the costs of staying in this dispute?

What do you need from the other person before you can move on?

Can you influence whether you will get what you need from the other person to move on?

Is there any way you can be the bigger person and move on without getting what you need from the other person?

Is there *one thing* you can do to remove some of the tension from this dispute?

What is your action plan to remove some of the tension?

Breaking down a fight to separate the negative emotion from the fight itself will provide you with insight about just how simple most fights are in content and in their solution. The negativity surrounding a fight is often blown out of proportion compared to the precipitating event. The simple act of separating emotion from content allows you to deal with the subject of the fight once and for all and move on.

Have patience with yourself, and with each other. Give yourself and your spouse the benefit of the doubt when it comes to the argument itself, and try to get to the root of the problem. "We fight about the kids' backpacks every time I pick them up after their time with you. Is there something you are upset about that I should know about?" You may not be the appropriate person to help your spouse with his feelings, but acknowledging it will shift the dynamic of the conflict. Acknowledging your own fear and being willing to show your vulnerability can also help. "I'm having a hard time with the financial cutbacks we've both had to make, too, and wanted you to know I've given up playing golf every weekend to put that money toward the repairs for the house."

As you listen to your spouse talk about a hot-button issue, listen for shame and trauma. Breakthrough moments can happen if you allow your spouse some leeway in her emotions. Underneath most anger is a cry for help. Remember that you are seeking to create a win-win situation for everyone in your family, so hold on to that goal. See what you can do to get underneath your spouse's complaints to help her heal. Maybe you don't even need to give in on

SEEKING PROFESSIONAL HELP

If you suspect your spouse has an addiction to a substance or behavior, or a mental health problem, be sure to seek help so you can get the support you need in dealing with the situation. These are serious issues that only a professional can diagnose and treat. Conversely, just because your husband is moody does not mean he is bipolar. A wife who is self-centered is not necessarily a narcissist. We have a greater awareness of many of these personality disorders as they are destigmatized and talked about in pop culture. That doesn't give us a license to diagnose others based on symptoms we saw on a prescription drug commercial.

something tangible like money or the dining room furniture; maybe she just needs to hear you say you are sorry this is happening. An apology can go a long way toward solving conflict, and many people are reluctant to give an apology because they see it as a sign of weakness. The hot button issue could represent a hurt that has been going on for a long time in your marriage. Give the person you once loved an opportunity for final closure on these issues wherever possible.

Aikido Response

One counterintuitive yet effective way to avoid conflict is to use a principle from the marshal art of aikido. In aikido you use your opponent's energy to work to your advantage. When you apply aikido to a conflict, you recognize that there is more strength in working with your spouse than against him. Allow the conflict to rise without getting defensive. Do not attack back. Acknowledge your spouse's concern, remembering that listening is not the same as obeying. This will throw him off base because he is expecting you to yell back.

> YOUR SPOUSE: I am so sick of you sending the kids back to me all hyped up on Sunday nights.
> YOU: Wow, I have really made you mad. Tell me more. How do they act when they get home?

or

> YOUR SPOUSE: You cannot call me at work to make changes in the parenting schedule. You are putting my job in jeopardy.
> YOU: I am so sorry! I had no idea. Is it the fact that I change things that makes you mad or that I call you at work? Can I email you? Is there another way I can communicate with

you if I have a change that won't get you in trouble with
your boss?

Listen hard and use as many open-ended questions as you can
to get your spouse to tell you everything she has to say and get it
all out. Listen with detachment yet without dissociating; stay alert
and present. Making your spouse feel heard will do a lot to defuse
the conflict. This demonstrates that you are not automatically
rejecting her feelings and that you want to understand the problem
so you can help solve it.

We often use blame, shame, or guilt to push back in an argument.
"It's not my fault the kids are so tired. You signed them up for sports
and after school care because you work too much." Make a deal with
yourself that you will no longer blame, shame, or guilt your spouse.
If he tries to blame, shame, or guilt you, say, "It's time for us to
stop shifting blame and take responsibility for ourselves." Instead of
blaming, ask questions to detoxify your issues and get the information you need to solve the problem: "Do you think the children are
involved in too many extracurricular activities? Would you like them
to be home more after school? Do you think they are enjoying their
sports and lessons? Or should we consider hiring a sitter?"

Staying on Course

> Courage doesn't always roar. Sometimes courage is the
> little voice at the end of the day that says I'll try again
> tomorrow.
>
> —MARY ANNE RADMACHER

Congratulations on the progress you've made toward making
your divorce work. You've created a mission statement. You are

mastering the peacemaking skills you learned with the 8 keys to resolving family conflict and the 8 peace practices. And now you have set your emotional GPS to goodness, steering you toward your best self. Take time to notice how good you feel about yourself. Celebrate what you are accomplishing and all the good you are bringing into your sphere of influence.

In the next chapter, you'll take a look at what you want next for your life and your self, and begin to set specific goals leading you toward more personal happiness and peace.

CHAPTER 6

What You Want Now

To be natural is such a difficult post to keep up.

—OSCAR WILDE

Divorce will completely redefine life as you know it. On the famous Holmes and Rahe Stress Scale, divorce measures 73 "Life Change Units," second only to death of a spouse, which measures 100. Here's the good news: You are the decision maker for many of the life changes that your divorce brings about. You are already committed to divorcing peacefully and respectfully. So along with the trepidation, allow yourself to feel excited and hopeful about the new life you are about to design for yourself.

Many divorcing couples assume their lives after divorce will be determined by a judge, based on what they are entitled to by law. Why anyone would leave such an important set of life decisions to a stranger, even a smart stranger, is a mystery to us. Even if you make imperfect decisions, aren't your choices about your life and destiny better informed and more sensible than those made by someone else?

A stranger doesn't have to determine the future for you, if you and your spouse can come to a settlement that you both agree on. In some states you don't have to go to court at all, and in others you just show up for a simple acknowledgment that you have an agreement. And if you need help coming to this agreement, there are lots of cost-effective people to go to for help, like mediators, collaborative lawyers, and counselors.

There may be other concerns at work, though. Most couples anticipate that they each will get about 50 percent of the marital pie and are worried that half a pie won't be enough for them. So what the law defines as "fair" doesn't always feel satisfactory. What you have to learn is how to make the pie bigger—that is, enlarge the range of alternatives so that everyone's needs are addressed and met to the greatest possible extent.

This chapter will help you define what you want for yourself and your family in your newly single life. At this point in your process, however, *you do not have to think about the particulars of your divorce settlement*. It is way too soon. In order to make a bigger pie, you'll need more information.

We are culturally indoctrinated to think the goal of a divorce is to take each other to the cleaners. By definition, that's lose/lose, and you are not going to divorce that way. You are going to go into your settlement discussions with an expansive attitude, knowing that there are countless ways for both you and your spouse to *get your needs met* and to meet the needs of your children.

It may be tempting to scheme how you can walk away with everything, but that's counterproductive. Now is the time to think seriously about what you really want—and need—in a concrete way, not as a way of extracting revenge on your spouse. We'll talk specifically about how to negotiate and finalize your settlement in chapter 10, "Negotiating Your Settlement," but that's where you end, not where you start.

You begin by defining your personal goals and priorities. You want to think first and then act. The best settlements are created using a measure-twice, cut-once approach. When you figure out first what you really want and need, even if your spouse isn't completely on board, you will inevitably save yourself tens of thousands of dollars and spare your family from the toll of home wreckonomics. See? Your pie already got bigger.

Spend Some Time Alone

Divorce can be a very lonely time and you may be tempted to fill your days with busywork, friends, family, and other distractions. But it is important for you to spend time alone because it:

- Helps you overcome your fear of being alone after so much time partnered with your spouse and provides the opportunity to cultivate a sense of privacy

- Gives you time to do some soul-searching as you think about the end of your marriage and learn from the problems that led up to it

- Helps you begin to own up to your role in the breakdown of your marriage and forgive yourself for what's happened

- Gives you space to reflect on any remaining disputes brewing between you and your spouse

- Helps you rediscover your uniqueness and identity totally independent of your spouse, your family, and the community at large, because your individuality may have become lost in the marriage, or in the weight of the breakdown

- Allows you to manage your hurt and anger and recover your sense of rationality about your divorce

Most important, use your time alone to make those determinations about what it is you now want and need, and why, because you will, in fact, be dealing with two divorces: the legal one and the emotional one.

The legal system expects your divorce to be a business deal, but you didn't get married as a business deal. That's where the disconnect between the legal system and the real meaning of the end of a marriage begins. This disconnect is where too many couples get into trouble—innocently and unwittingly.

Right now, you need to focus primarily on the emotional stuff—the reasons *behind why you want what you want*. If you try to jump right into the mechanics of the settlement without addressing the emotional piece, you'll end up with needless conflict in your settlement, probably racking up huge legal fees, losing personal control of the situation, and with a judge making the final decisions for you.

In order to most effectively handle the emotional side of your divorce, you will need to articulate your goals and develop a unique vision plan for what you want. Everything in this chapter will lead you to create this plan, and set you up for effectively negotiating your settlement—and for the rest of your life.

Emotional Readiness

Understanding *why* you want what you want will help you feel empowered so that, from a sense of lack or a place of fear, you don't have to resort to grubbing for every little thing you can get.

And you will come to realize that you do not have to get what you need and want at the expense of your spouse and children. Your emotional readiness will allow you to determine your true needs, wants, and desires for your new life and to create a new life of happiness for yourself.

Consider the following questions *before* you set out your goals:

Are you ready to commit to being fair?

Do you understand that it's counterproductive just to say you want *everything*?

Are you ready to talk about your needs and goals yet, or are you still too angry?

Do you feel you have the ability to assert your needs, or does that terrify you?

Do you acknowledge that what seems fair to you may not seem fair to your spouse?

Can you be honest with yourself about whether you have a hidden agenda to punish your spouse through the settlement? Can you let that go? Or at least try?

Do you understand that in order to be treated fairly you must be ready to treat your spouse fairly?

Are you ready to hear what your spouse wants, and why?

Are you ready to see your spouse's requests for what your spouse wants or needs rather than your spouse being out to get you?

Do you really want to end the fighting and make your divorce work?

Do you feel like you have been using the 8 keys to resolving family conflict and the 8 peace practices long enough that you won't be baited or goaded?

Are you ready to try to bring out the best in yourself and your spouse rather than the worst?

Are you ready to take on new roles that you may not have embraced during your marriage: breadwinner, housekeeper, accountant, or whatever?

Do you feel ready to care for your children without your spouse there to assist? And do you feel ready to be alone while your spouse cares for your children?

Do you really feel ready to accept your divorce?

If you answer no to any of these questions, you may not be entirely emotionally ready to proceed. But how can you get there? Take the time you need to be ready to answer yes to all of these questions before you begin your settlement discussions. The discussions and exercises in the following chapters will help you move through the emotional issues that may be blocking you from being ready to divorce. Come back to these questions after spending time with the concepts in each chapter.

Personal Responsibility

You have committed to coming out of your marriage happy, healthy, and whole. One of the biggest factors in your ability to get there is the degree to which you are able to take personal responsibility for what goes on in your divorce and your life after. Many people think personal power is the ability to strong-arm others to get what they want. It isn't. Power and responsibility are really synonymous. You have power over what you take responsibility for. If you have lived with a victim mentality up to now, personal responsibility may seem like a burden, or something that's impossible to achieve. It isn't a burden and it isn't impossible; it is where your treasure lies. People who take responsibility for their lives:

- Know they are responsible for their choices and the direction of their lives

- Don't blame others for their choices

- Know they are in charge of their thoughts and feelings

- Don't blame their parents or upbringing for who they are today

- Don't blame their spouse entirely for their divorce

- Realize they have a choice about how they respond to any situation, regardless of how negative that situation may be

- Know they are responsible for their own self-esteem and don't need compliments to feel good about themselves

- Take good care of their physical and mental health

- Play to their strengths

- Are aware of their weaknesses and compensate for them in ways besides leaning on others

- Let go of hurt feelings through forgiveness

Your divorce will be a struggle. You will have good days and bad days. You will always have a choice about how you respond on bad days. When you are tempted to take the low road, blaming

BE A HERO

Read through this list of statements and contemplate how many of them feel true for you. The items cover the complete emotional landscape from big life changes to seemingly mundane concerns. How many of these statements are true for you? Get a sense of places in your life where you feel like a victim and contemplate how you can begin to take more personal responsibility.

- I see how the choices I made in my marriage led me to divorce.
- I am responsible for our divorce just as my spouse is.
- I know that if I am feeling bad or negative, I can change my thoughts.
- My mood doesn't depend on my spouse's mood.
- My parents did the best job they could raising me and I'm thankful to them.
- My spouse did the best he or she could in our marriage and getting married was not a mistake.
- No matter how awful someone is being, I always have the choice to take the high road.
- I am careful not to get too down on myself.
- I try to make healthy choices about what to eat and to get enough exercise and rest.
- I understand I am under a great deal of stress right now and do what I can to reduce it.
- I do not engage in self-destructive or reckless behaviors.
- I am aware of things about myself I need to work on and am improving in those areas.
- I do not hold grudges.
- I am in charge of my life and don't need anyone to intervene and fix me.
- I know I can rise to whatever challenge life has to offer.
- I don't consider my marriage a failure.
- I am grateful for my life and look forward to what being single has to bring.

someone else for all the horrible things that have happened to you, consider the unbecoming traits of victims and ask yourself if you want to be that person. Victims are people who:

- Want someone else to fix them
- Think life is unfair and see no reason to try to take control and move forward
- Think they are a failure or a loser
- Feel too exhausted to rise to the challenge of their problems
- Find the world to be scary and negative
- Think that nothing is their fault because they simply are the way they are and can't change

Keep It Real

Commit to authenticity. The ability to reveal your true feelings and desires results in a more successful healing process, more accurate goal setting, and ultimately a win-win settlement. As you get ready for your divorce:

- Be honest and transparent.
- Do not guilt, manipulate, or force your spouse to bend to your desires, and do not allow your spouse to do that to you.
- Be clear about your needs.
- Be clear about your spouse's needs.
- Be clear about the children's needs.
- Allow each other to show you are in pain.

- Resist the temptation to stir up pain and anger.

- Hold a safe space for secrets and wounds.

- Hold a safe space for guilt and shame.

- Disagree respectfully.

- Try your best not to get defensive.

Setting Personal Goals

You are preparing yourself to set goals for your life based on knowing what you want and, more importantly, *why you want it.* Here's the reason.

Remember your aim is to make your divorce work for everyone in your family: you, your spouse, and your children. Your settlement isn't going to be all about compromise between you and your spouse where each of you feels like you must give something up so the other can have what he wants and vice versa.

Always keep in mind that *your* divorce is about making the pie bigger. Focus on *why* you want what you want (and understand the same about your spouse) so that you can see what's really

KEEP IT REAL FOR A WEEK

Practice keeping it real by telling nothing but the truth for an entire week. You don't have to hurt anyone's feelings. (If a friend asks if you like his tie and you don't, tell him it suits him and ask him where he got it.) Say yes to others' requests only when you mean yes. Let your no mean no and stick to it.

important and open up all the possibilities for both of you. But it all starts with interest-based negotiations. This is why you need to identify your interests now, rather than later. These interests will inform your goals.

As you articulate your goals, keep the following in mind:

- Understand that some of the things you want may not be reasonable or rational: revenge, reparation for hurt feelings, an apology, or relief from shame, guilt, embarrassment, or public perceptions of you. Be honest with yourself if you are having these feelings, because if you don't confront them, they could come out as passive aggression. Your objective is to move past this negative, counterproductive thinking as soon as you're ready.

- If there is anything you feel you are owed by your spouse either because you were married or as a result of getting divorced, don't keep this as a secret agenda or it will backfire on you. Did you forgo your own college degree to put your spouse through school? Have you given your spouse everything he or she ever wanted and feel your spouse has a hand out wanting more? What will satisfy this feeling of being owed something? You don't necessarily have to tell your spouse this; it might be better dealt with in therapy, writing in your notebook, or talking with a trusted friend. However, it is important for you to know it so you aren't punitive in your goal setting. You are going to deal with your negativity toward your spouse and not use your settlement (or continuing the conflict) as a way to act that out. You will use the techniques you learn in this book to forgive and move on. You will come out of your marriage with little or no unfinished business.

- Set your goals based on what you need and deserve. Don't base your demands solely on what you think you might be entitled to by law or what you saw your friend get. You want to feel good about your settlement. You want to feel like you received and took what you needed and deserved, yet not at the expense of your spouse (which may indirectly affect your children). It is in your enlightened self-interest that your spouse is also satisfied with the ultimate agreement, because a satisfied spouse will be more cooperative and more likely to abide by the promises made in the settlement agreement. Setting your goals is not about whether your needs are legitimate or not.

- Consider the values associated with your needs. These are the beliefs and principles you hold dear. If you conflict with your spouse in these areas, it may be one of the reasons you are divorcing and make it hard to come to a settlement. Did you sacrifice any of your values in your marriage? What can you do to make sure you hold on to what you value most regardless of what your spouse does, so you can regain a sense of yourself that may have been lost in your marriage? How can you do this without being defensive or intractable? How can you show respect for your spouse's conflicting values? *You don't solve value conflicts. You can only navigate around them and agree to disagree.* At the same time, don't forget to look beneath your professed goals to find the values that you and your spouse hold in common. This is the best way to expedite your negotiations—making the pie as big as possible.

- Identify what you consider to be fair based on your personal standard rather than a "legal" one (what a court would do) or a formulaic 50/50 split (which is not always possible). You do not have to go to court, unless you can't settle on your own. You decide.

- Separate your needs from your desires. A need is something that is essential to your well-being. Differentiate what you really need from things that you want but that are nonessential.

- Identify the needs in which you are emotionally invested. Take the time to write down the emotions associated with those needs. Give each of your needs a ranking of 1 to 10 so you will know your priorities and where you might have some wiggle room. You will want to be able to talk about these needs neutrally without getting overwhelmed. It is perfectly legitimate to have feelings about your personal belongings, Grandma's silver, or your first copy of *On the Road*, but getting overly emotional will not serve you in your settlement discussions. Always keep in mind that you are not responsible for identifying your spouse's needs. Try, however, to anticipate them as much as possible. This is good practice for the time when you sit down together to work on your settlement and must take your spouse's interests into consideration.

- Use words carefully. As you think about what you want next, try not to use the word "but." "I'd love to go to school, but I am too busy." As soon as you throw the word "but" into the equation, your mind closes to finding possible solutions. Use the word "and" instead. Saying "I'd love to go to school and I am too busy" leaves your mind to sit with the conflict and not dismiss it. This makes it far more likely you will be able to think of a creative way to rearrange your schedule to fit school in.

- Also try not to use the word "should." Use "get to" instead. "I really should start taking better care of my body if I want to date again" becomes "I'm so excited I get to go to the gym and work on my fitness." This technique helps your mind look at goals as exciting opportunities for growth and change rather than drudgery imposed on you from an outside authoritarian figure. And if you're not really feeling it, fake it until you make it. Once you get to the gym and start working out, you'll be glad you're there.

- When you are contemplating goals, aim high and wide. Don't rule anything out no matter how silly or impossible it seems. You can refine your goals as you go. This is not the time to think small. Consider the things that you don't like about your life right now that may have contributed to the breakdown of your marriage. Some basic goals may even seem counterintuitive or selfish. This is a time of major upheaval and change. If you could change anything in your life right now, what would it be? Some of your goals may include things like:

  - Cutting back on work if you've been using it to numb yourself or avoid your spouse.
  - Improving your appearance and getting in shape, even though you weren't able to find the motivation to do that for your spouse.
  - Quitting smoking or drinking, now for yourself, even though your spouse nagged and begged you to do it for years.
  - Not getting a job right away because you are scared out of your mind.
  - Relaxing and taking some time out for yourself. You spent more than a day getting into this situation, and it's going to take more than a day to get out of it. Taking fifteen minutes or fifteen hours (or even fifteen days) for yourself won't set you back in the long run.

As you set your goals, you may get in touch with some feelings of resentment or contempt. You could blame your spouse before. Soon it will be your life separate from your spouse, and you will have no one to blame but yourself. Set goals to specifically tackle what's holding you back.

Some people experience a high level of anxiety as they work on their goal setting. You may find that you have one overriding fear that looms in your mind, preventing you from thinking constructively about your interest-based goals. As you work through your goals, if you become stuck on one thing, it may stop you from moving ahead. At some point during your divorce, you may find that you are unable to think straight because you're so scared that the worst possible scenario will become a reality. Let's face it, threats like "I'll make sure you lose everything" and "You'll never see the kids again" are very common in divorce. Maybe you have your own worst-case scenario. Either way, facing up to the worst thing that could happen is an exercise that will allay your fears—or at least you will be mentally prepared for the catastrophe. Either is better than no plan at all and letting the worst outcomes of divorce overwhelm you like a tsunami.

Coping with a Catastrophe

The best way to handle any problem is to break it down into its smallest parts and then determine what you can do to solve it, step-by-step. Only then can you start to change the way you think about even the most overwhelming issues.

What's the Worst That Could Happen: Betsy's Story

Betsy and Frank had been married for ten years when Frank initiated their divorce. Betsy had seen it coming. Frank's behavior had become erratic for several months before he served her divorce papers without even telling her he was going to file. This was after a year of fighting over and over again about how much Frank resented Betsy for sitting home, doing nothing but spending his money, while he was out sacrificing to earn it.

"I'll make sure that you lose everything," Frank told Betsy.

Betsy wasn't sure if her husband's threat to cut her off and leave her with nothing was real or not. But she certainly felt more than a little intimidated. She wanted to get past this fear that had all but stopped her from working out what she really wanted. Betsy thought about the prompts in the next section to get in touch with her biggest fear and face it on paper, so she could at least soothe the fear of being unprepared should the worst actually come to pass. She wrote the following in her notebook:

My worst fear is that I actually will lose everything in this divorce. And I can't imagine anything worse. At least not legally. I could get cancer or my parent could die, but bankruptcy is about as bad as it can get legally for me at the moment. I think that there's maybe a 30 percent chance of this happening. And in my heart, I don't believe that it will really happen. I feel like I don't really know my husband anymore, and what he is capable of. He certainly is angry enough to do something pretty bad. But he's always been very financially responsible and bankruptcy would hurt him, too.

I barely got any sleep last night. Maybe I should take a nap. I could also get a massage, or call a friend. I will make another appointment with my therapist. I'd feel better if I wasn't alone. Maybe I should go to the dog park and spend some time. I just need something to help me calm down and think about this rationally.

The next time I start getting really upset about anything I'll know that it probably has to do with my fear of losing everything. So I don't have to work myself up into a real state before I call my mom.

If my mom or my friends aren't available to talk on the phone the next time I'm feeling this way, I can practice the deep breathing exercises, go for a walk, and then buy myself a fancy cup of coffee at that quirky coffeehouse downtown.

If I come to a dead end and just don't know what to do, maybe I can find a support group on the Internet. Maybe my friend Jill, who is always so poised, has an idea. My cousin is an attorney. Maybe I ought to call her.

Honestly, I am not sure what I can do to prevent this from happening. I know that there are some financial records in the garage. I'll photocopy them just in case. Maybe I should speak with an attorney before this goes any further—I'll make an appointment now so I can ask about what recourse I have if my husband does try to grab everything.

I now know that I have some resources and alternatives. I can consult with an attorney, or call my accountant. I can look at the self-help divorce books at the library or at the bookstore. If I take the records to a quick copy place, I can get them copied and take my time looking at them before I have to make a decision. Maybe I should find a financial advisor who can help me with them.

If my husband did leave me with nothing, it would be pretty hard. But money isn't everything. And at least we don't have kids to support. I can get a job and work my way out of any hole I find myself in. I have supportive friends and family and they can help me get through this, emotionally if not financially. Plenty of people have started over.

I'm within fifteen credits of graduating college and I've always wanted to be a teacher. Maybe now's the time. My friends and family (okay, not every friend and family member) will help me if I ask. I could move to my friend Jean's house—she got divorced two years ago and knows what I'm going through and maybe she'd rent me a room for a while, until I get back on my feet.

But if I find that I'm just not coping well emotionally—which is much more likely than starving or being homeless—my friend Rachel, who went through this last year, can probably help me figure out what to do. She's pretty sensible. And I know that the local psychological association or my health insurance company can recommend a therapist if my friends don't have suggestions.

Writing about her biggest fear in her notebook helped desensitize Betsy. She became more detached and logical when it came to thinking about her future. She also used the breathing exercise when she felt panicky and thought about the best (realistic) outcome for her situation rather than spiraling out of control.

What's the Worst That Can Happen: Your Story

Is there a catastrophe looming in your mind that is driving you to distraction? Would you be able to think more clearly if you didn't have so much fear about this horrible thing that might come to pass? Writing down your biggest fear is a way to gradually and gently expose and desensitize yourself to it before it happens (if it ever does). You can come up with a potential solution so you aren't filled with anxiety wondering and worrying about things that may never (and probably won't) happen.

When you make decisions from a place of confidence rather than fear, you have a far better chance of averting catastrophe than if you get all worked up and stew.

Ask yourself the following questions about your worst fear and then write about them in your notebook, like Betsy did. The more detailed and imaginative you can be in your description, the more aspects of your fear you can expose yourself to.

- What is my worst fear?

- Is there anything worse that can happen?

- If so, what is it?

Ask yourself the first three questions over and over again until you have exhausted your list of "worst" things.

- *Now* what's my worst fear?

- What's the likelihood that it will actually happen? (Express this as a percentage.)

- What's the likelihood that it won't happen? (Express this as a percentage.)

- In my heart, do I believe that it will really happen?

If it seems unlikely that your worst fear will happen:

- What can I do to feel calmer about this situation right now?

- Now that I'm calmer, how can I stop myself from going to this dark place again?

- What are the resources I can use now to help me stop thinking this way?

- If I don't have any ideas, who might help me with this?

If it seems likely that your worst fear will happen:

- What can I do to prevent this from happening?
- What are the resources I can use now to prevent this from happening?
- What can I do to cope with this if it does happen?
- What are the resources I can use now to help me cope if this does happen?
- If I don't have any ideas about what to do, who can I turn to who can help me with this?

Be patient with yourself. Do what you can do. Some days you will feel better and be more productive and open than others. Be honest with yourself about what you are ready for and try to do your best with each day. Your new life will be developed through your living it, so think of it as a journey rather than racing to get to the destination.

Play to your strengths. What did you want to do when you were a child? Is there a talent you have been ignoring that you'd like to develop? What makes you feel good about yourself?

Get out of your own way and be patient. A change as drastic as a divorce isn't going to resolve itself overnight. Also, sometimes it seems like nothing is happening to move you toward your goals and then you reach a critical mass and experience a growth spurt.

Areas of Goal Setting

You can use the categories in the vision plan listed in the next section to write your goals for the immediate, near, middle, and long term. Before you begin, consider these specific areas you will need to address so if you need to go back to resolve some outstanding issues, like some of those raised in this chapter, emotional or otherwise, you can do so before you start.

- Protection of the children. The greatest gift you can give your children is to reduce the level of acrimony in your divorce. *How will you show your children that you love them and the divorce is not their fault?* Make this your top priority.

- Logistics of the kids living in two households

- Running two households from your current income

- Funding the separation period

- Establishing your budget

- If one spouse is unemployed, how will that spouse transition into finding a job? Does that spouse need some money in the meantime? For how long? What arrangements does that spouse need to make to get on his or her feet?

- Child support: What are the immediate, near-term, and life-long expenses associated with child rearing and how will you handle these?

- Fair division of property (house, cars, etc.)

- Are there household goods you want because you have emotional attachment to them?

DARREN'S VISION PLAN

Darren was married to Karen for fifteen years. They had three children, ages twelve, nine, and five. He discovered she was having an affair when he received an email from Karen's lover's wife informing him that the affair had been going on for a year. Darren was devastated. He traveled extensively for his career, which gave Karen the time, opportunity, and reason for feeling neglected and turning outside her marriage for romance and attention.

Though Darren still loved Karen, he was so hurt by her affair that there was no chance of reconciliation. Plus, her lover was leaving his wife and planned to continue his relationship with Karen. Darren read through the prompts for the vision plan later in this chapter, and wrote up his goals in each area. When he was done, Darren was confident that he had thought about his future in every facet of his life. This really reduced his stress. It also helped him get over Karen more quickly because he had a definite idea for how he was going to take care of himself rather than counting on her, since he couldn't anymore. Darren wrote his vision plan in his notebook. He set goals for his new life and then identified each as a *need* or a *desire*. Then he ranked each on a scale from 10 (don't need it very much) to 1 (must have this need met). This helped Darren set his priorities. Doing so will help you set your own priorities, too.

I. Coming Clean

I feel that I am owed an apology from Karen for cheating on me. She has not apologized yet because she claims I deserved it because I ignored her and spent all my time at work. I don't know right now if I'll get what I want. I've told her she owes me an apology but it's always been in the middle of a fight so I am not sure if she even heard me. And, honestly, I don't think that I can let it go right now. I need Karen to acknowledge how much pain she caused.

II. My Standard of Fairness

I don't think that we really need to go to court to settle the divorce. I think what is fair is meeting the needs of my entire family, starting with the children. I'm super mad but I have definitely decided that I don't want to use the divorce to get back at Karen. I have my pride.

III. My Interest-Based Goals

FOR THE PROTECTION OF THE CHILDREN

I want to protect my children because I love them more than life itself and don't want them to suffer from our divorce. This goal is a need with a 1 ranking.

My goals for the children in the short term:

- They accept the divorce with hope for a better home life.
- Their schedules aren't interrupted.
- They are supported in breaking the news to their friends.

My goals for the children in the middle term:

- Child support that covers their expenses.
- A parenting plan that meets their needs and is flexible enough to accommodate the children as they grow and change.
- The children feel at home in both houses.

My goals for the children in the long term:

- My spouse and I never involve the children in our disputes.
- We are entirely comfortable in public as a divorced family.
- My children see that divorce was the best option for our family at the time.

LIVING APART

I want to set up two households for our family that feel as homey to each of us and the children as possible. This need is a need with a 1 ranking.

My goals for the households in the short term:

- Security deposit plus first and last month's rent paid on an apartment for me.
- Furnish the apartment with furniture from the basement and fill in with pieces purchased from a thrift store.
- Stay well under budget during the setup time so we save assets to use toward the divorce.

My goals for the households in the middle term:

- I will stay in an apartment for the first year so I have time to think about what I want.
- The children will decorate and set up their rooms so they feel at home in both places.
- Duplicate the key children's items in both households to reduce shuffling back and forth as much as possible.

My goals for the households in the long term:

- I eventually buy a house once I am certain of what I want.
- Both households live within their means.
- The children refer to both households as "home" rather than "Mom's house" and "Dad's house."

CO-PARENTING

I want to be a part of my children's lives on a daily basis, even when they are staying at my spouse's house. I want my parenting to be constant and seamless. This is something that we all need. This is a need with a 1 ranking.

My goals for co-parenting in the short term:

- Meet together with a counselor to establish an interim parenting plan.
- Tell the children (together) that the final decision will be up to Mom and Dad, but that we want their input.
- Test the parenting plan for a few weeks or a month to see if it is working and let everyone know their thoughts and feelings will be considered so speak up about what they really want.

My goals for co-parenting in the middle term:

- I communicate with my children daily in some form like email, text, or phone call.
- The children feel safe and comfortable and we follow whatever schedule we set.
- The children feel organized and prepared for school and their activities no matter which parent they are with.

My goals for co-parenting in the long term:

- The children feel equally bonded to both Mom and Dad.
- The children feel proud of interacting with Mom and Dad in public, even though we are divorced.
- The children are never used as spies to find out what is going on in the other household.

CONTACT WITH MY FORMER SPOUSE

I want to be cordial and businesslike with my spouse at first, with perhaps a friendship developing later on, but not now. This is just something on my wish list for now but isn't necessarily a priority. I need some time to get over the affair. This goal is a desire with a 5 ranking because it is something I know we'll really have to work on. I'm willing to give this a lot of leeway.

My goals for contact with my former spouse in the short term:

- Minimal at first so I can emotionally separate from the relationship.
- Email, call, or text to make an appointment to have a conversation longer than fifteen minutes.
- Email or text with information rather than call, to avoid conflict if at all possible.

My goals for contact with my former spouse in the middle term:

- Open lines of communication to be friendlier after the first year.
- Discuss the possibility of spending some holidays together depending on how things are going.
- Meet together with a counselor after the first year to see how we are progressing and identify issues that are coming up again or not healed yet.

My goals for contact with my former spouse in the long term:

- We are good friends.
- We have moved past anything negative that occurred in our marriage or divorce.
- We use our intimate knowledge of each other to be supportive of each other in our new lives.

RELATIONSHIP WITH FORMER IN-LAWS AND MUTUAL FRIENDS

I want to have an excellent relationship with my former in-laws and mutual friends I shared with my wife. But this is something that I think may come along eventually so I am not investing too much energy here now. This goal is a desire with a 6 rating. My in-laws and I agreed to give each other some time to come to terms with the divorce, so I can put this on hold.

My goals for a relationship with former in-laws and mutual friends in the short term:

- Let them "pick" who they want to be closer to at first and give them some time to get used to our divorce.
- Let them know we are having a peaceful divorce so they don't need to fear being put in the middle.
- Be cordial and warm with everyone.

My goals for a relationship with former in-laws and mutual friends in the middle term:

- Watch for which relationships naturally fall away and let them go.
- Never, ever bad-mouth or gossip about my spouse or our divorce.
- Spend time with in-laws and mutual friends separately or at a party, but not as a "couple."

My goals for a relationship with former in-laws and mutual friends in the long term:

- They never feel imposed on by our divorce.
- They never need to pick sides.
- They feel entirely comfortable with my spouse and me, individually or together.

MONEY

I want my wife to feel supported in the first few years of our divorce but to also know that being single means she will be responsible to earn her own money and support herself. I can't say this is a priority right now. This goal is a need with a 5 ranking. I understand I am going to have to wait for some of the financial details from my divorce to shake out before I can have a complete financial picture.

My goals regarding money in the short term:

- Give my wife spousal support to cover her expenses and leave her with a cushion so she can find a job without worrying.
- Make it clear to her that she will need to live within her means and establish a budget.
- Explain that there will be enough extra money in the initial spousal support payments that she could potentially save some of it, but that I am not going to manage her money for her.

My goals regarding money in the middle term:

- My former wife is working and I pay child support but not permanent spousal support.
- I continue earning to my potential and spend however I want to without having to answer to my wife anymore.
- I feel satisfied that what I did for my wife in the settlement was fair and if she ends up blowing her money or not getting the pay she wanted for her job, that is her responsibility.

My goals regarding money in the long term:

- I retire on time.
- I have money saved for my children's college.
- I have never had to give my wife extra money due to her irresponsible spending, and our finances have remained separate, as they should be after a divorce.

MY HEALTH AND WELL-BEING

I want to take care of myself so I look and feel the best I possibly can for my age. I can put a personal plan into action but I am not really setting this as a priority at this time since there are more pressing things to worry about. This is a desire with a 4 ranking. I am going to give myself time to set realistic goals and be gentle with the changes I need to make.

My goals for my health and well-being in the short term:

- Abstain from drinking for 6 months altogether to make sure I am thinking clearly and not self-medicating.
- Have a complete physical to see if I have any medical issues to deal with.
- Do some research to find out my ideal weight and body mass index and see how far off I am.

My goals for my health and well-being in the middle term:

- Eliminate refined sugar and processed carbohydrates from my diet completely.
- Discover two or three exercises that I enjoy and can stick with and incorporate them into a sustainable routine.
- My body mass index is within the "normal" range and I have treated or am treating my medical issues.

My goals for my health and well-being in the long term:

- I am in excellent health.
- I look and feel terrific.
- I am highly satisfied with my health and well-being and proud of the way I care for myself.

MY EMOTIONAL STATE

I need to feel good about my decision to divorce and proud of the way I handled myself. There are so many really important things that I'd like to accomplish but this is definitely up there. This is a need with a 1 ranking. I think that keeping this in mind will inform everything I do.

My goals for my emotional state in the short term:

- I am able to cope with my fear, anger and grief.
- I don't act out.
- I don't make a fool of myself.

My goals for my emotional state in the middle term:

- I'm able to let go quickly and am happier than I was in the later part of our marriage.
- I'm not afraid to admit I am happy in these unfortunate circumstances.
- I feel stable.

My goals for my emotional state in the long term:

- I am happier than I have been in years.
- I am at peace.
- I respect and admire my wife and am glad for the years we had together.

MOVING ON TO A NEW RELATIONSHIP

I want to find love again with no drama from my marriage to interfere. This is a desire with a 3 rating. I don't plan on dating right away.

My goals for moving on to a new relationship in the short term:

- I don't want to date for the first year.
- I want my children to feel comfortable when I do start to date.
- I do not want a new girlfriend or someone I am dating to support me in my divorce. I will handle this on my own.

My goals for moving on to a new relationship in the middle term:

- I want to date women who respect my co-parenting relationship.
- I want to date women who are stable and not looking for a lot of excitement (partying, drama, etc.).
- I'd like to date around quite a bit and not move directly into another long-term relationship.

My goals for my moving on to a new relationship in the long term:

- I would love to remarry.
- I want my former and current wives to get along well and not just tolerate each other.
- I want to be very supportive of my former wife if she decides to move on and find a new spouse also.

MY ATTACHMENT TO THINGS

Item	Emotional Attachment
China	Belonged to my mother
Car	I won it in a sales contest
Artwork	Painted by a local artist who I love
Stove	I took a cooking class and it is my passion
Vanity	I bought it used and restored it
Blender	My deceased aunt gave it to us as a gift

YOUR VISION PLAN

Use the following prompts to write up your vision plan in your notebook. Your vision plan will help you clearly identify what you want and why you want it. Writing out your goals also helps make them seem more real—and gives you the opportunity to take your time to think about each one. Label each goal that you identify as a *need* or a *desire*. Then, rank it on a scale from 10 (don't need it very much) to 1 (must have this need met). Doing so will help you set your own priorities.

This is the biggest thing we have asked you to write in your notebook. That's because it is so all-inclusive. Don't feel like you have to do it all in one sitting. Start where you feel like starting and take your time. This is your vision plan for everything that's important to you. This is your chance to go back and be the person you always knew you could be, despite your divorce.

I. Coming Clean

Feeling that you are owed something could hinder you from meeting your goals if you let this sense of entitlement, whether justified or not, piggyback onto or hide behind other problems. Deal with it directly when you feel ready.

- Do I feel I am owed something by my spouse either because we were married or as a result of our divorce? (If the answer is no, move on to the next prompt.)

- What is it?

- Is it likely I will get what I want so I can move on?

- Can I let it go without getting what I want from my spouse?

II. Standard of Fairness

As previously discussed, you will want to identify what you consider to be fair based on your personal standard rather than a legal or commonly accepted one.

- Do I feel that I need to go to court to settle my divorce?

- My standard of fairness will be based on what factors?

III. Interest-Based Goals

Now that you have come clean about any hidden agenda you may have and calibrated your standard of fairness, set interest-based goals in the following areas:

FOR THE PROTECTION OF THE CHILDREN

What are my goals for the protection of the children? Are these goals *needs* or *desires*? (Rank each from 1 to 10.)

My goals for the children in the short term . . .

My goals for the children in the middle term . . .

My goals for the children in the long term . . .

LIVING APART

What are my goals for figuring out how to live in two households— right now and for the future? Are these goals *needs* or *desires*? (Rank each from 1 to 10.)

My goals for the households in the short term . . .

My goals for the households in the middle term . . .

My goals for the households in the long term . . .

CO-PARENTING

What are my goals for co-parenting? Are these goals *needs* or *desires*? (Rank each from 1 to 10.)

My goals for co-parenting in the short term . . .

My goals for co-parenting in the middle term . . .

My goals for co-parenting in the long term . . .

CONTACT WITH MY FORMER SPOUSE

What are my goals for having an ongoing relationship with my former spouse? Are these goals *needs* or *desires*? (Rank each from 1 to 10.)

My goals for contact with my former spouse in the short term . . .

My goals for contact with my former spouse in the middle term . . .

My goals for contact with my former spouse in the long term . . .

RELATIONSHIP WITH FORMER IN-LAWS AND
MUTUAL FRIENDS

What are my goals for having an ongoing relationship with my former in-laws and mutual friends from my marriage? Are these goals *needs* or *desires*? (Rank each from 1 to 10.)

My goals for a relationship with former in-laws and mutual friends in the short term . . .

My goals for a relationship with former in-laws and mutual friends in the middle term . . .

My goals for a relationship with former in-laws and mutual friends in the long term . . .

MONEY

What are my goals concerning money? Are these goals *needs* or *desires*? (Rank each from 1 to 10.)

My goals regarding money in the short term . . .

My goals regarding money in the middle term . . .

My goals regarding money in the long term . . .

MY HEALTH AND WELL-BEING

What are my goals for my own health and well-being? Are these goals *needs* or *desires*? (Rank each from 1 to 10.)

My goals for my health and well-being in the short term . . .

My goals for my health and well-being in the middle term . . .

My goals for my health and well-being in the long term . . .

MY EMOTIONAL STATE

What are my goals concerning my emotional health? Are these *needs* or *desires*? (Rank each from 1 to 10.)

My goals for my emotional state in the short term . . .

My goals for my emotional state in the middle term . . .

My goals for my emotional state in the long term . . .

MOVING ON TO A NEW RELATIONSHIP

What are my goals for moving on to a new relationship? Are these goals *needs* or *desires*? (Rank each from 1 to 10.)

My goals for moving on to a new relationship in the short term . . .

My goals for moving on to a new relationship in the middle term . . .

My goals for my moving on to a new relationship in the long term . . .

MY ATTACHMENT TO THINGS

In your notebook, also list household items to which you feel emotionally attached and which you would like to take with you as part of your settlement. Next to each item, write why you are emotionally attached to it. This is only a wish list at this point. Understanding your emotional attachment will help you in your negotiations.

Knowing why you want something helps you understand how you may be able to meet this need in several different ways and still be satisfied.

Moving Toward Your Goals

You have just written out your interest-based goals and dealt with your worst fears. You are making your divorce work. In the next chapter, you'll see how important it is to walk your talk so all your actions are in line with your goals and objectives. Take time out to congratulate yourself and even celebrate. You have a lot to be proud of.

CHAPTER 7

Walk Your Talk

Nobody trips over mountains. It is the small pebble that causes you to stumble. Pass all the pebbles in your path and you will find you have crossed the mountain.

—JAPANESE PROVERB

Congratulations on your progress toward a peaceful divorce. Do not underestimate your pioneering effort and what you have accomplished so far. These achievements are huge and you're already on the road to a better life ahead.

You now have an understanding of the 8 keys to resolving family conflict, the 8 peace practices, why your marriage ended, and what you want your post-divorce life to look like and what your goals are to get you there.

Your challenge now is how do you walk your talk and translate what you have learned into actually taking the steps necessary to make your divorce work. Knowing what to do and actually doing it are two different things. It won't be easy and it won't be perfect at first, but you'll get there.

Focus on Your Intention for Peace

Walking your talk simply means you do what you say you are going to do. Once you have set your goals for a peaceful divorce and your new life afterward, how do you make sure you reach them? Walking your talk has nothing to do with pleasing others. It is a way of making sure you make good on the promises you have made to yourself. How do you motivate yourself to stay true to your intent in the face of the hurdles that appear in a situation as daunting as divorce?

Learning to live with your thoughts and actions focused on your goals is simple yet not easy. It takes some retraining, and no one can do it for you. Eventually you will feel comfortable enjoying a daily routine that is free of chaos, where your time is spent on projects and people that are in line with your values and goals. In time you will value your sanity above all else and preserving it will be second nature.

Start by trusting your will to do good. Not in a moral sense, per se. This is more about your innate tendency to want to be the best expression of yourself that you can possibly be. When you live according to your mission statement and goals, the quality of your experience will be so good that you will lose your desire for conflict entirely.

Conduct yourself as if you were being filmed for a reality TV show. What would you want people to see and talk about later? The truth is that you'd want the reality show about your divorce to be so boring that no one would watch. A boring divorce is a good divorce. Peace may not seem nearly as tempting as hacking into your spouse's email or lurking around on Facebook to see what she wrote on her old boyfriend's wall. But your family will benefit from its cumulative effect and you will spare yourself a lot of damage that comes with all that drama, which we will talk more about later in this chapter.

Peace is its own reward. Watch for the next time you are proud of yourself and how you handle a difficult and chaotic situation. Anchor to that feeling. Work it like a muscle and watch it grow. Conversely, be hypervigilant for the times during the day when your mind seeks something to intensify the thought or emotion you are experiencing. That's drama. Then just reject it. Just refuse to engage in it. Every time you refuse to engage in highly charged situations and with overly emotional people, you build a reserve of peace.

Instead of getting sucked into the chaos, use your favorite from among the 8 peace practices to correct your course. It's like training a puppy with positive reinforcement. The puppy needs something to chew on, but it can't be your good shoe. So you give her a toy instead. Do the same thing for yourself with your mind. It doesn't help to spank the puppy, and it also doesn't help to punish yourself. Good dog training is about leading, positive reinforcement, and correcting behavior. You must do the same thing to retrain yourself with your mind. You control your mind. If it needs some excitement,

WHAT I DID RIGHT TODAY

Take a moment each day, or even several times a day, to make a list of things you did right, situations in which you were pleased at the outcome because of something you did, and progress you've made, however small. This does not have to be "achieved world peace." Your accomplishments can be very simple, like "walked the dog for fifteen minutes instead of watching TV," "drank water instead of soda," or "praised a coworker in front of the boss."

Reflecting on positive things will change your mood, and over time, these reflections can have a huge positive impact on your frame of mind.

find a stimulating, positive, constructive activity like learning to rock climb or speak Russian rather than something destructive, like repeatedly calling your spouse and hanging up. It's up to you to re-channel thoughts into those that lead to actions, behavior, and the destination you really want rather than divorce devastation.

Be aware that some of your friendships may shift or naturally fall away if they have been based largely in negativity. With some people you might be able to say "I am not going to engage in nega-tive behavior anymore so please support me." With other people you will just have to refuse to engage and not say anything to them because they will try to sabotage you. If you have to let go of some negative, chaotic, or drama-filled friendships, then so be it.

Learn to value life as it comes and accept that not every moment needs to be fabulous for you to experience lasting joy and fulfill-ment. *Peace is not boring.* It is being fully alive and engaged.

Focus on Your Goals

There are countless ways to get knocked off track, many of which have to do with the popular misperception that acrimony is the nor-mal way of divorce. Having a peaceful divorce is counterintuitive, so you will need an internal countering force to help keep you on track.

Look at the goals you set for yourself in chapter 6. Break your goals down into smaller goals and focus on them one at a time. Revisit your most important goals every day. Reward yourself for the little accomplishments with things that further nourish (not deplete) you. Find healthy ways to generate an overall higher qual-ity of experience in your life rather than simply stirring up excite-ment. Satisfaction endures long after excitement fades.

Focus on your career. Enjoy a hobby you love. Spend time with people in nurturing, mutually supportive relationships. Don't let other people bring you down with their negative attitudes and issues. Choose positive entertainment. Don't let the media make you more anxious or depressed.

Don't procrastinate. It is actually more stressful and painful to *put off* doing something that you know will be good for you than to just sit down and get started. You can accomplish so much in just a half hour when you apply yourself. You want to try to make your positive actions become habitual. It takes practice to be firm yet gentle with yourself. It takes courage to cut out time wasters that aren't related to your goal.

Make a Bigger Pie

Always approach your goals in a way that is win-win for your entire family, whether you feel like it or not. Remember that it is in your own self-interest to have your spouse be easy to deal with, and it's easier for your spouse to be reasonable if you are reasonable first. Listen empathetically for what your spouse says he needs, because that is how you build the bigger pie. Put yourself in your spouse's shoes, not just your own, when searching for solutions.

Settling your divorce is about making sure your most important goals get met and that you compromise the least on them. The same is true for your spouse. When you identify both sets of goals, prioritize them, and then make trade-offs, the pie gets bigger, not smaller.

Be Mindful of Your Legal Settlement

Walking your talk in your legal settlement means that you approach it with a commitment to fairness, honesty, and cooperation. Discussing your financial settlement and shared parenting responsibilities will not be easy. You're talking about everything that means anything to you—your children, your financial security, the dreams you had for your marriage, and the death of those dreams. You will have strong feelings during this time. It doesn't help that the legal system asks you to get divorced as a business decision. You didn't get married as a business decision, so it probably feels odd to you to treat your divorce like the breakup of a corporation. So it's okay to feel upset and unnerved by the entire process. In fact, it's normal. The problem is that it isn't productive.

The best that you can do is to approach every step of this negotiation in a way that's consistent with your divorce mission statement. Know that your spouse is struggling with these issues, too, as is everyone else who's getting divorced. You're not alone, although you may feel very alone. But if you stay true to your mission statement, you'll be on the right path to getting through everything happy, healthy, and whole.

There's another reason to walk your talk in your legal settlement. You cannot achieve your legal settlement without your spouse's cooperation. As a result, the offers you make need to meet his needs and seem reasonable to him in addition to meeting your needs and priorities. You must learn to live independent of your spouse and set up your own life, but you may need to rely on your spouse and his cooperation if you co-parent or have any kind of ongoing relationship, like owning a home together or working at the same company. Your lives may still be intertwined through your families and mutual friends, too. Acrimony in your settlement will make the things that make life fun, like holidays, sharing friendships, and so forth, more complicated for everyone. So walking your talk is worth it.

Avoid Drama

Sometimes people going through divorce behave in ways that make a given situation seem much more important than it is. The following behaviors and the tone around them make the issue seem so pressing and imperative that it is easy to get sucked in:

- Yelling, screaming, and other conflict

- Lying or withholding information

- Having bad boundaries or letting other people's bad boundaries affect you

- Betraying a confidence (or other types of betrayal)

- Spying (driving by, looking at email or Facebook, etc.)

- Spreading rumors (about your spouse, in-laws, divorce proceedings, etc.)

- Exaggerating

- Being mean or cruel

- Playing the victim to illicit sympathy and attention

Your mantra is "I focus on the core values in my mission statement and goals." This means you stay away from the ultimate time, energy, and composure vampire—drama! Drama makes everything seem urgent, and it is tempting to get caught up in it. When it crops up (and it will), take a moment to assess where the so-called crisis fits into your goals and mission for your divorce. If spending time or energy on the situation demanding your attention doesn't help you accomplish your goals, don't take the bait. Don't lose your focus.

To preserve your sanity, you must learn to distinguish drama from something worthy of your attention. Drama can appear positive and exciting or negative and juicy. Be vigilant for extreme emotions in yourself and others. When you feel a body rush when faced with a situation, be on drama alert.

It is not uncommon for drama to manifest itself in situations like the following:

Elly's husband knew she was on thin ice at work because he kept calling her during working hours, which was affecting her performance. He did it anyway. His bad boundaries were drama.

A female friend of Fred's was Facebook friends with the man his ex-wife was dating. She gave Fred her password so he could log on as her and lurk on the man's profile. His spying was drama.

Marian's husband suggested she sell the house and divide the profits between the two of them equally, and she blew a gasket, lecturing him about how she deserved more because she was the one who cleaned the house for ten years while he was hardly ever home. Her exaggeration was drama.

Jim had another fight with his spouse. He headed to the bar and complained to the attractive bartender. His playing the victim to seek sympathy is drama.

When you look at these scenarios (and think of examples from your own life), how do they help accomplish the goals and mission of a peaceful divorce? The answer is that they don't.

These feelings and behaviors have been legitimized by media, especially reality TV. It's juicy entertainment. Drama produces a high, which makes the more mundane aspects of life feel flat, as though nothing significant is happening. None of this makes it okay for you to indulge.

It doesn't really matter why you may engage in drama, the key is to be aware that if you get sucked in by drama, you need to de-intensify your life and find more consistent balance.

DO YOU GET SUCKED INTO DRAMA?

Consider the following statements and ask if they apply to you. If you respond yes more frequently than no, chances are you are susceptible to drama and need to be more focused on your mission and goals—and leave drama to the stage and the reality shows.

Life with my spouse was flat and boring. I wanted more glamour than my spouse did.

I lie to my spouse because some things are just none of her business anymore.

My spouse really knows how to manipulate me.

I have checked up on my spouse to see if he is where he says he is going to be.

I have looked at my spouse's email without her knowing about it.

I have maintained some of our mutual friends as "frenemies" so I can pump them for information about my spouse.

I look at my spouse's cell phone bill to see who he is calling.

If I don't want to tell my spouse where I am going, I don't have to.

I have an online relationship with an opposite sex friend that my spouse doesn't know about.

I have a credit card my spouse doesn't know about.

PEOPLE WILL TALK

Anticipate that as part of the drama, everyone is going to have something to say about your divorce. In a perfect world, all of your friends, family, and coworkers would be sensible, supportive, rational people who would stick by you, not take sides, refuse to gossip, and be available to talk in the middle of the night. You need to be ready to deal with everyone else.

They Mean Well, But . . .

The first category to be wary of is people who mean well but who are not at all helpful. Maybe they take your side, no matter how preposterous your behavior: "You were totally justified throwing all of her stuff out the second-story window onto the front lawn!" Or maybe they got their legal education from a soap opera: "Once the judge hears your side of the story, your ex is going to have to volunteer for medical experiments he'll be so broke!" Their exaggerations are drama.

They may also appear to be slightly educated and knowledgeable about divorce. This is a dangerous category. These are your acquaintances and coworkers who have been through a divorce, or their best friend has been through a divorce. They'll make statements like "You're only going to pay $25 a week in child support" or "I got $500,000 in my settlement and so you will, too." Never mind that the person paying $25 a week in child support only earns $150 a week and that your friend who received $500,000 as a settlement had $1,000,000 in net assets and her spouse got $500,000 also. Your well-meaning friends left out those details, of course.

At least these people are trying to be helpful. You just have to keep this in perspective. They mean well, but if you listen to them, you're doing yourself a disservice. Their cheerleading and ill-informed legal advice means trouble for you if you pay too much attention to it.

The Haters

And then there are the haters. People who think that people who get divorced are weak, immoral, quitters, or worse. Don't buy into their melodrama, because anyone who tells you it's too easy to get divorced has never been divorced; nobody with half a conscience jumps into a divorce like it's going to be fun. People who get divorced really take it to heart. Nobody enters into this decision lightly.

You've probably heard all the arguments about why you shouldn't get divorced. If you haven't heard them, you're going to hear them, because some hater is going to make a list for you, trying to stir up drama. The problem is that this hater is probably someone close to you, someone whose opinion matters to you or who has influence over your life. Listening and being tempted to take that person's opinions to heart will make your life miserable.

Know in your heart that the hater's pronouncements do not apply to you. You wouldn't make a hasty decision. You've thought about this carefully and really tried your best to make your marriage work. And if the divorce wasn't your idea, then you didn't even ask for it. Maybe you would've hung in there longer, gone to counseling, tried everything to save your marriage, but it just wasn't your choice. The haters don't get this. But making you feel bad and passing judgment on your life is their drama. It doesn't have to be yours.

Responding to the Well-Intentioned and the Haters

Rather than succumbing to the urge to justify your divorce to people with their own agendas, you're going to walk your talk by taking personal responsibility.

If you've done something about which you feel guilty, you are going to apologize. If you've done something wrong, you are going to make it right and you're going to vow not to make the same mistake again.

You are going to be responsible all of the way through this process—to your spouse, to your children, to your family, to your job, to your community. You are going to handle this in the very best way possible. And when you make mistakes, or do something you regret, you're going to take responsibility for your actions and make things right.

You are also not going to cave in to your guilty feelings or your spouse's cajoling, unreasonable demands, or bad behavior. You are going to take the high road. And when you take the low road, you're going to get yourself back on the high road as soon as possible. You are going to be a responsible adult who handles adversity with maturity and respect for everyone involved.

Consider the person described in the preceding paragraphs, and imagine it's someone else. What right would anyone have to pass judgment on a person like that? What right would anyone have to say that that person is a quitter, a loser, or a promise-breaker? It's okay to ignore the haters.

Life is full of adversity. If your divorce is the first really stressful, bad thing that has happened to you, then you're lucky. Unfortunately, there are going to be plenty of other awful things that will happen in your life over which you may have very little control: death, illness, accidents, and wars. Fortunately, your divorce is a solvable problem. And the solution is largely based on your own behavior, which means that you control the outcome.

WHEN OTHERS FAIL TO SUPPORT YOU

When the people in your life who are supposed to support you during this difficult time don't support you, don't take it personally. It may just be their own drama at work. Consider the following:

- Your ex is very close with *your* family and they continue to include him in events, at times even excluding you. Are they

trying to manipulate you into changing your mind or punish you for getting divorced?

- Your best friend is in an unhappy marriage. When you tell her that your husband left and you're getting divorced, she stops talking to you. Could it be that she is jealous? Or simply incapable of admitting her own unhappiness?

- You're the first person in your very traditional family to get divorced. When you break the news to your family, they call you a failure, threaten to have your children taken away, and put you on the prayer list at church. Are they worried that they somehow let you down and that's why you are getting divorced?

Can you see that these people are basing their behavior toward you on *their* issues and not yours? When you can take yourself out of the equation, you can get some perspective and see how counterproductive this kind of behavior is.

But it's harder when it's you and your family or friends. You believe that these people love you and care about you (and they do, they are just misguided at the moment), and you know you care about them and what they think.

There are so many common remarks that people make to others going through a divorce that it isn't hard to create a list of these, many of which will certainly resonate with you. More important, however, is your response. While the scenarios may not play out exactly as they appear in the following examples, these reasonable responses to unreasonable remarks will no doubt give you food for thought.

REMARK: Why are you getting divorced? Mark is such a good father, person, and provider. There must be something wrong with you.

RESPONSE: I think Mark is all of those things, too. It just didn't work out. There is nothing wrong with either of us. We tried our best.

REMARK: You didn't try hard enough to stay married.

RESPONSE: We both did everything we could to try and save this marriage. I'm disappointed we're divorcing, too, but it's just the reality.

REMARK: If you really loved your children, you'd stay for their sakes.

RESPONSE: We are going to do everything we can to make sure the children are fine. We are committed to making sure that they have two loving homes and two committed, cooperative parents. We can love our children and can take good care of them even if we're divorced.

REMARK: You've broken a promise you made in front of God and all of our relatives.

RESPONSE: I hate the idea that I've broken that promise, too, but sometimes things like this are unavoidable.

REMARK: You dropped out of college, too. I guess you're just a quitter.

RESPONSE: Getting divorced isn't about quitting. This has been a very difficult period of time for both of us. I know our decision is surprising news to you, but we've been working on this for a very long time, trying our best to figure out how to keep this together. Sometimes you just can't make it work, and to keep working at something that's not working is worse than quitting and moving on.

REMARK: Nobody else is ever going to love you. You're divorced. Now you're damaged goods.

RESPONSE: I don't know if I'll find love again. I just know that staying in this marriage isn't right. I don't agree that I'm damaged goods or that no one will love me again. I've learned a lot from the challenges and mistakes in this marriage and when I'm ready to move on, the right relationship will happen for me.

CONTAINMENT

One way to avoid drama and to keep your sanity intact during your divorce is to practice containment. This means that you keep what's happening in your divorce to yourself. Of course speaking with a therapist or counselor can be an excellent investment of time and money during your divorce. But burdening your family and friends with every detail can, more often than not, scatter your focus. You want to avoid the drama of presenting yourself as a victim and being helpless. You want to maintain your focus so that you gather insight about your personal responsibility and power. No one can change what is going on in your life except you. On a very practical level, the sane thing to do is be a grown-up, take personal responsibility for what goes on with you day to day, stay in your own business, and keep moving forward.

Here are some tips for practicing containment:

- Don't tell the random person next to you at a luncheon, your hairdresser, or the person behind you in line at the coffee shop all about your horrible divorce.

- Keep your spouse's secrets. If she has had an affair or a drinking, drug, or gambling problem, don't blab. Let your spouse deal with it on her own terms. Don't punish her by trying to ruin her reputation.

- Next time you have a fight, contain yourself. Don't immediately pick up the phone and call your best friend to get her to validate what a monster your spouse is.

- Stay out of other people's drama. You don't have time to get into it anyway. If two mutual friends are fighting, stay neutral.

- If you have friends who thrive on drama, you may have to let go of some of those relationships for now. You must conserve your energy for your own situation. Getting sucked into other people's problems is a way to avoid having to work on your own.

- If you really need to vent and tell someone, consider asking one friend you respect. This should be a person whose opinion you trust, who has given you permission to use him or her as your venting buddy and vowed to help you keep your goals, mission, and perspective during this process. Vow not to overwork that person.

- Consider speaking with a professional counselor, clergy, divorce support group leader, or other healing-minded professional who will keep you on track.

Avoiding Distraction: Bianca's Story

Bianca was married for seventeen years when she and her husband divorced. She experienced a lot of frustration with interruptions from her friends that she simply didn't have time for anymore now that she was a single working mother. Bianca thought about the prompts in the next section and then wrote about a common distraction in her notebook to help her see a way to deal with it and alleviate her frustration. Here is her notebook entry:

> I was helping my daughter with her homework when my friend Michelle called crying because a man she had a date with last Friday hadn't called her this week. Michelle does this frequently and my listening to her doesn't seem to help at all. I care about her and she is important to me as a friend, but solving her problems really has nothing to do with my goals right now.
>
> I was feeling like I could tell her I was busy and get off the phone until she said "I really need you right now because this is so painful, I can't bear it." I had a hard time saying no to her because she was so upset.
>
> I got frustrated because I wasn't helping my daughter or Michelle. When I hung up the phone with her, Michelle was still crying, and our conversation didn't do anything to make her date call so it was a complete waste of time. My daughter was frustrated, too, because she was eager to get her homework done and play.
>
> From now on I am going to screen my calls and not pick up the phone when I am helping my daughter with her homework. I think I'll take Michelle out to lunch and gently tell her that I am super busy with my new life as a single mom and I don't feel like I can support her through the ups and downs of dating right now. I'll offer to schedule time with her for a long lunch once a month to talk about things like that.

Avoiding Distraction: Your Story

Think of a situation you wish had been handled differently. Did you get sucked into a fight which didn't need to happen? Did you let someone else's idea of what's important overshadow your own goals and priorities?

Below are some prompts you can use to write about it in your notebook. As you assess what distracted you, stick to just the facts. Stay out of the story and the emotional charge associated with the facts. The drama lies outside the facts, and that's what you are seeking to trim away in your examination of the event.

- What happened that got you off course? Just the facts.

- What were you doing when the interruption occurred?

- Was the interruption important to you and your goals?

- Was it important to the other person?

- What specifically made the interruption seem so urgent and important that you got sucked into believing it deserved your attention?

- Did you really attend to either situation (your goal or the interruption) in a productive way?

- Do you really think you helped solve the problem or helped the person who interrupted you?

- Did the interruption help you reach your goals in your divorce?

- Were you aligned with your divorce mission statement?

- What could you do next time to stay on course?

Disengaging and Setting Boundaries

Remember that when you say no to something not in line with your mission, you say yes to your win-win divorce and your healthy life afterward. Disengaging from people, situations, and behaviors that drain you will contribute to your reserve of inner peace because you will respect yourself and others more.

- If a person or situation is sucking away at your time and energy, you must protect yourself and your family.

- Disengaging may upset others at first. In the long run, they will respect you more, or fall away from your life. Do you really want "friends" who don't respect you?

- Disengaging is the right thing to do. Your time and energy are valuable, and once they are spent, you can't get them back.

- Be hard on the problem, not the people. You don't have to get mad to set a boundary. You are not saying no to the person, just to their unreasonable request.

- Use the breathing exercise to help you relax before you disengage. If you allow yourself to get worked up, you may end up feeling bad and caving.

LET YOUR NO MEAN NO

Disengaging from drama and setting boundaries means your no means no. It's ironic that two-year-olds have no problem saying "No!" and "Mine!" all the time and yet grown-ups find it challenging. Here are some ways to politely disengage:

- I hate to keep you on the phone, so let's check the time and limit this to twenty minutes.

- No, thanks, but I'm honored that you asked me to be a Boy Scout troop leader.

- Sorry, but I won't be able to pick your children up from after care this time.

- I'm sorry, I can't. [With no explanation.]

- Please don't email me or call me at work. I've set that as a personal rule for myself so I can get that promotion I've been trying for, but let's get together soon so we can really catch up.

- I think it's great you are all taking Deb to lunch and treating her for her birthday. I thought I'd get her a card on my own.

- I enjoy our conversations and would love it if we could set a phone date so we won't have so many interruptions.

- Thanks for the invitation but I'm booked that weekend. Have fun!

- No.

You get the gist. There are a million ways to disengage. If you feel guilty when you do so, you could be suffering from the disease to please and it may take you a little time to get used to how weird it feels to put *your mission and goals* ahead of others'. There is an old saying, "Fill your own cup first, and feed others from the overflow." Keep that in mind. It's all about having good boundaries.

SELF-SOOTHING

It's always easier to walk your talk when you are having a good day. *Why, yes! All of the good things that are happening are a direct result of my efforts!* Easy. You'll need to be equally prepared to take care of yourself when you are having a rough day so you don't spiral into a pit of despair, of blame, shame, and guilt.

How are you going to take care of yourself and stay on track when things get rough? You won't have your spouse to rely on anymore. You can't rely solely on your friends all the time or you may jeopardize your relationships. Walking your talk includes cultivating the ability to soothe yourself when you are feeling overwhelmed and tempted to give away your power by making a source outside you culpable for something negative you are experiencing.

It's important to choose techniques that will work for you, plus you may have ideas of your own. Try:

- **Venting.** As emotion builds up, we have a natural need to give voice to it. Venting can be healthy in small doses. Choose a few friends you can vent to and ask them to agree to listen once or twice for a short time each. Be sure to also ask your friends to be honest and to let you know if your venting is allowing you just to stay stuck rather than to blow off steam. If you find yourself venting repeatedly about the same issues, you may want to seek the help of a professional counselor to get sound psychological advice and be fair to your friends. And if all of your friends are saying the same things, which sound productive and nurturing, ask yourself why you're not following their solid advice.

- **Visit online communities or chat rooms.** There is an online forum or chat room for just about every problem you can think of. Joining one of these groups can be another way to give voice to your issues. Just be careful of the limitations of online communities and honest with yourself about whether you are really soothing yourself through satisfying mutual exchange, or staying stuck and just spouse bashing.

- **Write in your notebook.** By writing in your notebook, you can vent without overburdening or ruining friendships. You can be fully self-expressed on paper without ever showing it to anyone. Save your writing and come back to it later to see if problems repeat themselves, get worse, or if you are making progress. Or tear the pages out of your notebook and burn them as a literal gesture of your letting go, once you are ready.

- **Relaxation techniques.** Use the breathing exercise as often as possible to help you relax on a daily basis. There are also thousands of relaxation DVDs and CDs. Find one that suits you and use it when you are upset. Cultivating the ability to calm yourself down is the biggest investment you can make in yourself during this stressful time.

- **Spa treatments.** A spa treatment isn't bona fide self-soothing, because it involves paying another person to assist you in relaxing. However, a manicure, pedicure, massage, facial, or new haircut can really help take the edge off and boost your physical appearance, too.

- **Exercise for endorphins.** Go for a brisk walk around the block, hop on a treadmill for ten minutes, do some calisthenics, or anything else you can think of to get a quick endorphin release plus feel your body relax after a period of intense exertion.

- **Distract yourself with something engaging that you enjoy.** Choose an activity that will require your full concentration so you can lose yourself entirely. What activities did you enjoy as a child? What hobby did you do before you got married that got left by the wayside?

- **Focus outward on something rewarding.** The best way to stop feeling sorry for yourself is to focus on someone else. Talk to a friend about his problems without bringing up yours. Do volunteer work. Practice random acts of kindness.

- **Count your blessings.** List all the things you have to be thankful for. Include at least five good things about your marriage and your spouse. Also list five positive things about getting divorced.

- **Get organized.** Rearrange your furniture and clean your house. If that seems like too much for now, organize some personal papers, or start with one cabinet or even one drawer. Your environment is a reflection of your inner state of mind, and one can affect the other. It's hard to stay in a bad mood when you are tired from a hard day of house chores and can fall into bed with the smug knowledge that your closet is clean and that you donated things to charity.

- **Laugh.** Rent a funny movie or go to a comedy club. Laugh at yourself whenever you can.

Coming Out Happy, Healthy, and Whole

The key to walking your talk is to make every decision in your divorce based on your core values. You can influence your divorce in a positive way, even if your spouse doesn't cooperate. You don't have to simply accept your fate or react badly to an unfortunate circumstance. If you walk your talk, you will get to happy, healthy, and whole.

START TODAY

Critical in walking your talk is to be happy, healthy, and whole *today*. Don't wait for some time in the future when it will magically happen for you. Being happy, healthy, and whole will happen as a direct result of your thoughts, attitude, and behaviors. You will improve your life by focusing at every stage in your divorce on what you can change and accepting what you cannot change. You don't have to be perfect all the time. Every step in the right direction, no matter how small, will create measurable, cumulative, positive results.

Unhappy, Unhealthy, Incomplete: Three Stories

In addition to identifying your goals, it is also valuable to look for areas where you are currently unhappy, unhealthy, or incomplete, so you can address these areas right now and watch for them as potential pitfalls where backsliding can occur. Reflect on each area of concern and how it shows up in the way you think, act, and talk. Then, think about ways you can change your thinking, behavior, and language *right now* so they are more in line with your core values and so you can deal with what concerns you most right away. Below, you will read the way three divorcing people— Lisa, Joe, and Mack—addressed their issues in an effort to get past them and on to their new lives.

Each person read the prompts in the next section and thought about where they were unhappy, unhealthy, or incomplete. The following are entries from each of their notebooks.

I Am Unhappy: Lisa's Story

Lisa was married to Brent for seven years when he asked her for a divorce. They didn't have any children, but they were planning to when they got married and it just never happened. Lisa always dreamed of being a mother and assumed the role of housewife, with Brent supporting her, in anticipation of starting a family.

When Brent asked for the divorce, it became immediately clear to Lisa that she was going to have to work to support herself, which made her very sad after she had spent the last seven years at home rather than working on her career.

She wrote the following in her notebook:

I am unhappy feeling like I have not accomplished anything professionally and now I have to go back to work. I feel inadequate and closed down around people I perceive as successful. I get defensive with anyone who wants to talk to me about looking for a job, even when they are being helpful.

I'll change my thinking about this by focusing on accepting that my feelings are natural and I can move through them. I'll identify the skills that I already have that could translate into a potential job for myself and take pride in them. I'll reframe my ideas about never having been successful into thoughts about embarking on an exciting path toward success. When I feel jealous of someone else who is already successful, I will remind myself that if that person can do it, so can I. Their success is proof that I can be successful, too.

I will not cut myself down in public or mention to other people that I feel like a professional failure. I'll engage in conversation with people who I think are successful, ask them about their success, and how they may have struggled to gain self-confidence. I'll use an upbeat tone and positive words to describe what I'm going through to myself and others in an exciting way, rather than presenting myself as a victim.

I can do things like meet with a career counselor or an employment agency to seek help. I'll update my skills as best I can under the circumstances. I'll reward myself for little successes like learning a new software program. I'll make sure my résumé is up-to-date and then try to get as many interviews as possible. I refuse to take rejection personally and remember there may be many reasons why I don't get a particular job that have nothing to do with my skills or abilities.

I Am Unhealthy: Joe's Story

Joe was married to Marlene for ten years and they had three children. Marlene said she had been unhappy in her marriage for years and was sick of taking care of everyone with no time for herself. Joe was not happy either, but he was willing to sacrifice passion for the comforts of living with someone who provided a nice home to return to after his long days working. Not used to making his own meals, he began to feel the effects of eating a poor diet rather than the three nutritious meals Marlene provided in his marriage.

Joe wrote the following in his notebook:

Since I moved out of our house and into an apartment, my eating habits have become really bad. I think that's why I have such low energy. I don't even feel motivated to grocery shop so I keep eating take-out. Plus, I've gained weight and spend a lot more money on food than is in my budget.

I really have to eat more nutritious meals as not only a health concern, but as a way to stay within my budget, and as a role model for my children, who I think may be falling into these bad habits as well. I'll stop complaining about how sluggish and fat I feel—and do something about it.

My first step will be to get to the store and shop for fresh food every week and stop going to restaurants or ordering take-out so often. I will pack my lunch for work the night before. I can also try to use a food journal to keep track of what I am eating—and how I am feeling when I indulge in junk food.

I Feel Incomplete: Mack's Story

Mack was married to Sally for twenty-five years when she asked him
for a divorce. Though Mack knew they were both suffering with
the boredom their marriage had sunk into, at least it was familiar.
After Sally moved out, Mack found himself feeling very lonely even
though he couldn't really say that he missed Sally. It's not like their
relationship was very engaging when they were together.

To explore why he was feeling incomplete, Mack wrote the following in his notebook:

> I feel really incomplete without my wife. Even though our mar-
> riage is finished, I miss the companionship. I hate the way I
> am clingy and constantly looking for reassurance from my
> sisters and platonic female friends that I am still a catch. I'm
> embarrassed to attend social functions alone. Sometimes I cry
> in front of my children, which I know alarms them.
>
> I have to start thinking differently about being newly single
> and take this as an opportunity to get to know myself, sepa-
> rate from being a couple. If I focus on the good things that
> come with being alone—like being able to watch three football
> games in a row and not answer to anyone—I think I'd be hap-
> pier with my lot. But I'll also remind myself that I am not the
> only single person my age, and that there are others who've
> lost their spouses under more tragic circumstances.
>
> Talking about myself as a bachelor rather than a divorcé
> actually makes me feel better—and not like half a couple. I
> won't talk about being lonely except only occasionally and
> with trusted friends. I'll also let my friends know that I am
> open to being fixed up!
>
> Even though I don't like it, I'll force myself to attend social
> functions on my own, and think of it as an adventure to meet

someone new (not necessarily a romantic interest) or just to people watch. I know several friends who've met people online using one of those dating services—I figure it can't hurt, and it's a lot easier at first than having to go to a mixer or hang out in a bar with all the youngsters. But, when I really think about it, now might be a good time to look into taking a carpentry class at the local community college—do something for myself and not just depend on someone else to make me feel human.

Unhappy, Unhealthy, Incomplete: Your Story

Writing out your own particular issues in your notebook is the best way to focus on what concerns you most—and to figure out what's holding you back. Now that you have read what Lisa, Joe, and Mack wrote in their notebooks, do the same thing with your areas of concern. Read through the list of prompts and be as specific as you can about the areas where you feel unhappy, unhealthy (emotionally or physically), or incomplete. Sometimes what's really bothering you most isn't even that difficult to remedy. Writing in your notebook will help you look at the way you act, how you think, and the language you use about yourself and your situation, and guide you to find ways to change your behavior. Here are some prompts to help you:

- Area of concern

- This manifests in my behavior in the following way . . .

- I will change my thinking about my concern in the following way . . .

- I will change my language about this concern in the following way . . .

- I will change my behavior about this concern in the following way . . .

Match Your Effort to Your Intentions

You now have everything you need to make sure your efforts will match your intentions. You've written out your goals and mission and also identified potential pitfalls ahead of time, so you can avoid them. You have examined where you feel unhealthy, unhappy, and incomplete and can focus on personally changing your life in these areas. You are hypervigilant for drama and how to set boundaries and disengage so that you can concentrate on the important things.

With these resolves in mind, you have set a course toward a peaceful divorce, but the powerful emotional forces of grief could still derail you. Learning to handle these feelings is the subject of the next chapter.

CHAPTER 8

Grieving the Loss of Your Marriage

Should you shield the canyons from the windstorms you
would never see the true beauty of their carvings.

—ELISABETH KÜBLER-ROSS

We can't tell you where your emotions come from or why you feel
what you feel. We can tell you that you will experience fear, anger,
and grief as you divorce. The better you can handle these feelings,
the better you will cope.

There is no way to make your divorce completely painless.
These feelings of losing control and being overwhelmed are normal. The good news is that you can do something about how you
handle those feelings.

Divorce is a very sad time for everyone involved. In many ways,
it is like a death. What started out as a big celebration filled with
high hopes is now ending with legal papers disposing of everything
you built together. It's healthy and natural to have strong feelings
and grieve the death of your marriage.

You will go through the same basic emotional phases of grief
during your divorce that you would concerning any other death,

stages that Elisabeth Kübler-Ross identified in her seminal work, *On Death and Dying*: denial, anger, bargaining, depression, and acceptance. There is so much to deal with in a divorce that you may feel you don't have time to grieve until the divorce itself is over. But if you can feel your loss now and express to yourself, your spouse, and others how sad you are, this will go a long way toward humanizing and normalizing your relationship. Making your divorce work includes recognizing and honoring that the emotional part of your divorce is as legitimate as, and perhaps more important than, the legal aspect.

Grieving the loss of your marriage is a process. The five stages of grief are emotions that many people feel during and after their divorce, yet everyone moves through these stages in his or her own way. The five stages of grief provide a context to help you navigate and understand your feelings at this time of upheaval. They can serve as guideposts yet aren't intended to explain away your grief via tidy categories. Movement through the stages is rarely linear, and it is impossible to put your emotions on a specific timeline. You may think you are through with one stage only to find yourself revisiting it several times. This is natural.

You are learning to cope with the loss of your marriage and all that it meant to you. Give yourself the time and space you need to sort through what you are feeling and deal with it when you are ready. Divorce, like your grief, is also a process, so new feelings may crop up as you make the decisions that move you toward your final settlement. When you know what to expect and that your feelings are normal, you can allow yourself to experience your grief knowing that it won't swallow you up into oblivion. Feeling what you feel and moving through the stages of grief are what enable you to finally reach the end stage, acceptance. Having strategies for understanding grief and loss will empower you when the going gets tough.

The first step in grieving is coming to terms with your own feelings about divorce in general. This will help you understand that the nature of your grief is not as simple as "I am sad my marriage is over." Your grieving process will be far more complex than garden-variety sadness. A person who has strong negative feelings about divorce in general, no matter who it happens to, may have more challenges in moving toward acceptance. Someone who sees divorce as an unfortunate but common rite of passage, which many married people experience, may be alleviated of the grief associated with thoughts about divorce being inherently bad or wrong.

Your Own Feelings About Divorce

As part of your own grieving process, you may have your own guilty feelings that divorce is taking the easy way out, that you'll doom your children to latchkey status and to struggling to overcome the challenges of a broken home, or that your breakup will fulfill any number of other widely held mythical beliefs about divorce. These feelings can be a hybrid of the denial and bargaining stages of grief. Remember that at your core, you are a good person who would not knowingly make an immoral or poor decision. *That's not you.* Just because others believe that divorce is wrong, or immoral, or easy, doesn't mean it's the truth. And you certainly don't have to make it your truth.

We do not see divorce as a moral failing. A divorce is just one of those awful things that happen. No one chooses to get married only to have it end in divorce, any more than anyone would choose depression or cancer. Making your divorce work is a way to create peace on earth, one family at a time.

The way you view divorce in general will have a huge impact on how you handle your own divorce. Perhaps the ideas have been handed down in your family for so long you never stopped to question whether they were true for you. Loosen your grip on thinking of divorce as something inherently bad and consider the possibility that although you couldn't make your marriage work, you can make your divorce work.

The Five Stages of Grief in Divorce

Let's talk about the five stages of grief: denial, anger, bargaining, depression, and acceptance, one by one.

DENIAL

In a divorce, denial often manifests as fear. Your reality is about to change drastically and that can be very scary. You may wish your divorce wasn't happening and that it would just go away. Perhaps you are so shocked you simply can't believe this is happening to you. This numbing aspect of denial in response to crisis is a valuable coping mechanism at the start of your grief process because it gives you time to come to terms with the unpleasant circumstances of your divorce and the realities of restructuring your life. But ignoring and denying your fears will not make them go away. As soon as you feel ready to recognize and understand that your marriage is in fact ending, you can move on to identifying and confronting your fear. Denying your fear will allow you to pretend everything's okay for a little while, but you will eventually need to face the reality of your situation.

Confronting your fear takes away its power and makes it less likely that the things you are afraid of will come to pass. Facing your fear means thinking through the worst things that could possibly happen and planning how you'd deal with them.

The two biggest fears we see in divorcing couples are "What will happen to my kids?" and "Will I have enough money?" Both fears are normal. The best news is that they're mostly unfounded. Or at least solvable.

The research shows that children of peaceful divorce do fine. Divorce itself does not hurt children. Since your divorce is going to be peaceful, your children are protected. Acrimony in divorce *and marriage* is what puts children at risk. Kids tend to believe what they see more than what they are told, and they learn by example. If you tell your children they are not responsible for your divorce and that you and your spouse still love them unconditionally and will be there for them *and then do that*, your children will do very well. If you make your divorce work, your children will thrive and even benefit from your example of calm, forward-thinking, goal-oriented and forgiving behavior.

Financial fears are often more real, especially because it's more expensive to support two households than one. So if money was already an issue, it's going to present even more of a challenge in your divorce. It can be scary too, if you haven't been actively involved in earning, saving, or budgeting money in the marriage.

Finances are also a source of many power imbalances for divorcing couples. You can use your divorce to change this dynamic. Don't just worry and point a finger at your spouse, saying that she is hiding money or not being forthright. Take control. You don't have to stay in the dark, and if you do, it's your own fault. It doesn't have to be that way. Being in the dark is a choice. If managing money is too scary, choose a financial advisor you trust implicitly and rely on her advice. From now on, you will be solely responsible for your financial future. You may for the first time ever have to budget to live within your means. Too many people get what they think is a nice settlement, blow it all in the first year, and find themselves in financial dire straits. Don't let that be you.

If you do not face your fears, they will either prevent you from doing something you really need to do, or cause you to do something you shouldn't.

As you face the unknown on the other side of divorce, you may experience one or more of the following:

- Fear of loss (children, spouse, extended family, friends, money, possessions, social status, role as wife, husband, sister-in-law, son-in-law)

- Fear of being alone

- Fear of having less personal security because you no longer have a partner

- Fear that you are a failure or something is wrong with you because you couldn't make your marriage work

- Fear that you are no longer attractive

- Fear of lack of control (especially if you feel like your spouse or attorneys are in control of the situation)

- Fear for basic survival issues (not enough money for two households)

- Fear of the risks you will need to take to start your new life

- Fear of telling your spouse how you really feel on issues that may affect your settlement and life afterward

- Fear that you won't get a fair settlement

Feeling all of these fears is normal. These are scary things to face. You are up to the challenge.

Dealing with Fear

If you are feeling paralyzed or overwhelmed with fear, the first thing to do is stop panicking. Use the self-soothing techniques from chapter 7, "Walk Your Talk," that work best for you.

When you are ready, here are some ways you can deal with your fear:

- Desensitize yourself by identifying your fear and saying it out loud.

- Make a beginning plan with small, easy steps you can take which will gradually lessen your discomfort until you have faced the issue fully.

- Recognize and list all of the ways in which your fear restricts you.

- Imagine all the ways in which letting go of fear will free you.

- If you are immobilized by fear of failure, list the things you've learned from past failures and how failure can serve as your ally.

Embracing Your Fears: Emily's Story

Emily was married to Oliver for thirty years when he left her at age fifty-five for a twenty-five-year-old. Emily understood that Oliver's affair was not the sole cause of their divorce, but that didn't make it any easier to accept that her husband was with someone so much younger than her, only underscoring all that was negative about her age and stage in life.

She had a hard time shaking her fear that because her husband had seemingly abandoned her for someone younger that meant she was destined to be alone. She struggled with thoughts about having given Oliver the best years of her life hoping they'd grow old together, only to be left single at the start of what was supposed to be their golden years.

Emily read the prompts in the next section and addressed her nagging fears. She wrote about her thoughts in her notebook as follows:

I am afraid that nobody will find me attractive at fifty-five and I'll sit home alone and never go out since I won't be able to get a date. If that happens, it will be bad, but it won't be the end of the world. At least I have my health.

In my heart, I don't believe that it will really happen—at least not completely. But when I ask myself what I can do to prevent it from happening, I have to admit that I can't help how old I am, but I can update my wardrobe and hairstyle, and learn how to use dating websites and social media so I can meet some new people. And I do know that I'm not the only person who's ever felt this way. There must be a group for dating over fifty or a support group somewhere.

I find that I feel bad about myself a lot. I know that I should stop saying I'm going to do something about my appearance and actually do it. Plus it's not all about appearance. I can be more outgoing at parties or even throw one myself. I have plenty of friends. I can also cultivate those relationships. It's not all about dating. There are other ways to have fun.

Now that I think of it, my friend Darlene is very social. She never seems to have trouble meeting new people and she dates a lot. In fact, she's older than me and heavier, too. I could ask her to help me. I know a therapist I could call and ask about a support group and I could also ask my Employee Assistance Program at work.

If my best friend told me that she was scared of the same thing, I would tell her that she was attractive and that she has a nice personality and that if she would just put herself out there that she'd meet the right person. And I know I really believe it about her, so I can believe it about myself, too.

Dealing with Fear: Your Story

When you articulate your fears, you start to change your mind-set from panic to problem solving. Use the following questions as prompts to help you begin to deal with and even embrace your fears and write about them in your notebook. This can be scary, so take your time. You can sketch your ideas out first and come back and flesh them in later when you are feeling brave.

- What am I afraid of?

- What will I do if it happens?

- If it happens, will it be the end of the world?

- In my heart, do I believe that it will really happen?

- Is there anything I can do to prevent it from happening?

- Is there somewhere I can go for support to help prevent it from happening?

- Is this a recurring fear that never gets resolved or addressed?

- If so, what can I do to stop that from happening?

- If I don't have any ideas about what to do, who can I turn to who can help me with this?

- If my best friend told me that he or she was scared of the same thing, what advice would I offer?

Facing Fear and Accepting Failure

Understand that failure or rejection is feedback to help you correct your course, not something inherently bad. If you are walking and have a pain in your foot, you stop and take off your shoe, find the stone, shake it out, and move on. You can do this with your mental health as well.

Feel the fear and do it anyway. Courageous people do not lack fear. They just do what they set out to do in spite of it. Courage grows as you use it. It doesn't make fear go away, it just loosens the grip of its immobilizing properties.

Think of an example of the time and energy you wasted worrying about something that didn't come to pass. Then think of an example of the way overcoming fears you have experienced in your life has contributed to the good in you today. What did you used to be afraid of and then overcome that made you a better person today?

Remember the times you have actually enjoyed fear and sought it out on purpose—on a roller coaster or at a horror movie. The fear you are feeling now is part of the ride of your divorce. Know that you will only feel it for a short while and then it will pass. Fear tends to come in waves and then dissipate. Anticipate this and allow for it.

When you are freaking out, let people you are close to know what's happening. They will want to be supportive, or you may want to suggest to them that they give you a wide berth. Your fear is not something to be shared with casual acquaintances, coworkers, or strangers. Use the peace practices that work best for you from chapter 4 to help calm yourself. If you find that you're repeatedly unable to get the fear under control, this might be a good time to make an appointment with a mental health professional or counselor.

Practice the breathing exercise to calm yourself down. Do it twice a day every day if you can. Remember there's a natural tendency to hold your breath when you are afraid, so make sure you breathe continuously, normally, and deeply *especially* when you are in a panic.

When you feel afraid, just be with it. Don't try to run away from it, control it, or sedate it. There is something under the fear for you to learn, and if you freeze up, you will miss out on that. Find a quiet moment after work or after the kids are in bed when you can acknowledge and address your fears.

After you have identified your fear and determined the ways you will deal with it *if* the thing you fear happens, focus on what you would rather have happen. Take action to alleviate your fear. What is one small, easy thing you can do right now to move in the direction of a solution?

Remember that words are important and that our attitudes strongly influence our behavior. How can you think about this fear in a new way so next time it crops up you will immediately have a way to stop and regroup: "I am afraid I will be homeless" becomes "I have enough money to live according to this budget for eight months and I plan to find a job within three, so I will be fine."

ANGER

Divorce anger can be particularly bitter, vindictive, punitive, and vengeful. It is also often expressed through the legal process, leading to prolonged emotional proceedings that can leave you and your family to deal with home wreckonomics.

You do not have to create a reason to justify wanting to leave your marriage. You don't have to be angry with your spouse and your spouse doesn't have to be a monster in order for you to have a valid reason to divorce. It may honestly be that things just didn't work out. It may be that you're unsatisfied and unfulfilled in your marriage. Divorces don't have to be full of fireworks in order to be the right decision.

Curiously, you may not recognize that your behavior or mood is based in anger at yourself, your spouse, other people who you feel interfered with your marriage, or at circumstances in your life that you felt contributed to your growing apart, like working long hours or having an unplanned child.

Dealing with Anger

Anger is an important and necessary part of your grief process. We live in a culture that fears anger, and we seem to know more about how to suppress it than how to feel it constructively. Anger can seem like it has no end, and your anger over your divorce can extend beyond just being mad at your spouse to include many other people, choices, circumstances, and relationships that you feel may have contributed to the end of your marriage.

At this point in your relationship, it is important for you to thoroughly acknowledge your anger. This means that you no longer expect your spouse to *do or say anything* to resolve your anger for you. You are divorcing and giving each other a clean slate. You may never get what you feel you need from your spouse, so you will cultivate what you need within yourself using the tools in this book. It's an unexpected luxury if your spouse does happen to help you resolve your issues.

If you allow yourself to feel the anger, it will ultimately move through you. Recognize when you are overwhelmed and wait for the anger to dissipate. Notice the thoughts you have during this time so you can get to the root of what you are feeling. To really feel your anger, first let it wash over you without trying to do anything to sedate or control it. Contain it and keep it to yourself until you are certain you are in control. You are in no condition to work with your anger until you can think clearly about it once the initial flash of emotion has passed. When you are ready to deal with it, consider:

- Sometimes it is good to vent. But venting can also reinforce the anger, so you should keep that in check. Do you really need to tell someone why you are so mad? If you do, tell a trusted friend and keep it brief. If you are grousing for the sake of grousing, it will probably do nothing more for you than keep you upset and overwhelmed.

- Write out all your angry feelings in a letter and then burn, delete, or shred it.

- Identify what triggers your anger: the tone of your spouse's voice, a gesture or face your spouse makes, certain topics of conversation. Next time, refuse to react in the same old way.

- Count to ten (or one hundred). Do the breathing exercise. Self-soothe in any way that takes you out of a flood of anger before you react in a way you will later regret.

- Keep children out of the conflict.

- Choose your battles.

- Scream in private.

- Get professional help with a therapist.

- Remember the old saying that when you point the finger at someone you are pointing three fingers back at yourself.

Overcoming Anger: Bill's Story

Bill was married to Cheri for twelve years before he filed for divorce. He and Cheri met in college. Bill went on to medical school and Cheri supported him. They had their first and only child when Bill was in his last year of residency. He made a fortune as a plastic surgeon, and when he told Cheri he wanted a divorce, she flat out told him she was going to take him to the cleaners and that he owed her for all the years she sacrificed for his success.

Bill had a lot of anger toward Cheri which had been building up long before the divorce. He saw her as already having rewarded herself for her sacrifices by spending money indiscriminately and without consulting him. He felt taken advantage of in his own family, which made him furious.

Bill wanted to overcome his anger so he could productively settle his divorce and effectively co-parent with Cheri. He read through the prompts in the next section and got in touch with the depth of his fury. Then, he wrote the following entry in his notebook:

I am angry that Cheri only thinks about herself and that she is giving me a hard time about division of assets in our divorce. It seems like she wants everything and I'm tired of it. But being angry doesn't really help me. It just makes me madder and madder every time I think about it. Maybe I am avoiding thinking about what it's going to be like when I'm single and no longer have her to complain about anymore.

I admit that what I am feeling may not be "healthy" anger and it's definitely taking over my life. She is selfish and I am right. In fact I've been angry about her selfishness for years. Just last night I woke up in the middle of the night thinking about it and getting mad at her all over again.

To make this situation better I just have to finish this divorce as soon as possible so that I can be done with her demands. But I really need to let go of this anger because it's not like she's going to change. She's been selfish since the day I met her. My being angry doesn't make her any less so. The more I think about it, the more I realize that's just who she is and she's never going to change. I need to accept that fact, even though I'm not happy with it. Then maybe I can stop getting angry every time she opens her mouth.

I don't really know what it will take for me to let go of this anger. It may take a while, but since I still have to deal with her as part of the divorce, I am going to formulate a settlement proposal and get it to her as soon as possible so that I can move past this. In the meantime I can focus on more positive things, like my fishing trip and our son's Little League play-off game.

She must be feeling miserable inside. I can't imagine how unhappy she must be to act like this all the time. So I'll try to remember when she's nagging me that she must be an unhappy person to behave that way and I'll refuse to react negatively to her unceasing demands. I can tune it out.

I don't want to burden other people with this but my best friend went through a similar situation last year. I'll call him and see what he has to say. There is also a support group at my temple for divorced and divorcing parents. Maybe I'll go one time. And, if none of the things I've thought of work, I'll talk to the counselor that my friend used during his divorce and I am sure there's a book on dealing with difficult people that I could read, or attend a seminar.

If someone in this same situation asked me for advice, I'd tell him that it isn't worth wasting his time or energy being angry. This situation happens to lots of people in their divorce; it always seems like the other person wants too much. I might also suggest that he really listen to all of her demands. Maybe if he listens to everything all at once and asks her why she wants what she wants she will feel that he does care about her needs—and maybe then she'll stop pushing so much.

Your Story of Anger

Bill's story allowed him to work through his feelings of anger. He used the questions that follow here as prompts to explore why he was so mad and what he could do to defuse his rage. He didn't necessarily respond to every question exactly as it appears, but these prompts gave him a framework for his own story. When you feel ready, contemplate the prompts with regard to your own anger and write your thoughts in your notebook.

- What am I angry about?

- What need does being angry serve for me?

- Is this natural, healthy anger, or am I letting it take over my life?

- Is there anything I can do to make this situation better?

- Is this recurring anger that never gets resolved or addressed?

- If so, what can I do to stop that dynamic?

- What would it take for me to let go of this anger?

- What can I do to help myself let go?

- Is there somewhere I can go for support to help me be less upset about this?

- If I don't have any ideas about what to do, who can I turn to who can help me with this?

- If someone else I know found themselves in the same situation, what advice would I offer?

BARGAINING

There will be times during your divorce process when you would give anything to be able to go back in time and do things differently. What if you had been nicer, more attentive, taken better care of yourself, or spent less money? Would your marriage have lasted? Perhaps you weren't sure about getting married at the time of your wedding and walked down the aisle anyway. What if you could go back and never have gotten married in the first place? What could you do or say to make your divorce go away?

Some bargaining may have to do with wishing you could strike a deal with your spouse. For example:

- Maybe I could put up with his overspending if I get a second job.

- If I helped her set up at the art fairs where she sells her ceramics, I could show her that I do care about her passion.

- His mother really wasn't any meaner to me than mine was to him.

- Her one-night stand with that guy on the business trip wasn't a full-blown affair.

At this point you may not really even want to stay in your marriage, you just wish with all your heart that this wasn't happening to you and your family. Your mind is overwhelmed with "What if . . ." questions. Bargaining helps distract you from the pain of the loss you are facing. It is a way to try to avoid having the bad things you don't want to happen occur.

Moving Through the Bargaining Stage

One way to move through the bargaining stage is to acknowledge and accept that you can't change the past. Vow not to make the same mistakes again. Reading this book is a good start.

Another element in moving past bargaining is to realize that many of the commonly held beliefs about marriage and divorce are myths, rather than truths. You may feel like wishing away your divorce because you buy into one of the following fictitious ideas about marriage and divorce.

MYTH: THE JONESES HAD A SUCCESSFUL FIFTY-YEAR MARRIAGE

There is a myth that the longer a marriage lasts, the better it is. We all know that isn't true, but the fairy tale spell of happily ever after is really hard to break after we grow up idealizing it our entire lives.

Just because a couple stays together until they die doesn't mean they had a good marriage. Plenty of couples sleep in separate beds, lead separate lives, or just go along to get along in quiet desperation. Some openly hate each other and fight daily, confusing their children about what love is and setting a poor example of marriage for them to follow. Other marriages involve substance abuse, mental cruelty or violence, or all of the above. So don't fall for the myth that just because people are married they're happy.

You can choose to look at your marriage as having been good for the number of years you were happily married and your spouse as having been perfect for you at the time. A marriage can be successful whether it lasts for four years or forty. What is important is the way you frame your marriage and the story you tell about it.

MYTH: DIVORCE IS AN EPIDEMIC

The fact is that people have been getting divorced, or wanting to, ever since the institution of marriage was created.

The truth is our society's norms and laws allow us to leave bad marriages, plain and simple. Divorce is not an epidemic or even a sickness. It can be a healthy option allowing people to move on from unions that are no longer satisfying and to find happiness, wholeness, and health.

Families are changing as our notions of relationships are changing. Yet what remains is that families are inherently and amazingly pliable and durable. Our ideas of who we consider kin are becoming more expansive as we open our hearts to ideas of "relatives" that go beyond the boundaries of our families of origin. Marriage and family don't automatically go together anymore. You can divorce and still preserve and even enhance your family.

MYTH: DIVORCE DEVASTATES CHILDREN

The single best indicator of how children fare in the wake of divorce is how conflict is handled by their parents. It is not *whether* you divorce that will affect your children; it is *how* you handle conflict.

In reality, a couple with children doesn't get divorced *from* each other, they get divorced *to each other*. If you have children, your divorce will change the configuration of your family, but you will still be family.

Divorce doesn't devastate children. Parents devastate children by constantly being embroiled in conflict. If you want to do right by your kids, it is up to you to make your divorce work.

MYTH: DIVORCED PEOPLE ARE FAILURES

More than half of all marriages end in divorce. Are all of these people failures? Of course not.

The most effective thing you can do to destigmatize divorce is to let the stigma end with you by handling your divorce well. Then, value your bi-nuclear family as much as you did your nuclear family by creating a fair settlement that works for you, your former spouse, and your children. Be good co-parents.

Rather than see yourself or your marriage as a failure, feel proud of yourself that you had the courage to end your marriage peacefully. How can your marriage be viewed as a total failure if it produced your beautiful children and made you a better person? And you can choose to see your divorce as a way to fix a home that was broken rather than as a process that creates a broken home.

Divorce is not a problem; done well, it is a solution. Most couples seeking divorce see it as the last possible option after much heartache and soul-searching. We are not going to reduce a divorce rate that has been stable for forty years. What we seek to do instead is reduce the negativity and recovery time associated with it.

Some of your friends and relatives may never accept your divorce. The values that we each hold about marriage, children, and family, and the history behind them, are loaded. That's just the way it is. It's critical that *you* accept your divorce and forgive both you and your spouse for ending your marriage. Your actions and behaviors during this process will also help others forgive you (even though there's nothing they need to forgive you for) and to adjust to the new reality.

DEPRESSION

Try as you might, you will eventually come to the realization that you simply cannot make your bargain go through. You can't do and say just the right thing that will change your spouse and instantly heal your marriage. No matter what deal you try to strike, real or imaginary, the sad reality is that you are getting divorced. This leads to the next stage in the grief process, depression.

Dealing with Depression

If you are depressed and sad, admit it, lean into it, and be with it. It is not bottomless. You are going to hurt for a while but not forever.

As time goes on, and your divorce is resolved, things will start to get back to normal—your new normal—and the good days will start to outnumber the bad.

There is a difference between simply being sad or temporarily depressed and clinical depression. The most basic definition of clinical depression is feeling so bad that you lose interest and take no pleasure at all in your life for two weeks or more, or you have feelings of worthlessness. If these statements describe you, please seek the help of a professional counselor who can determine if you are experiencing a natural part of your grief process or a more serious depression that should be treated medically.

For those moments when you feel overwhelmed with grief, one way of dealing with it is to simply remove yourself from the situation and be alone where you can cry or mourn until you have no more tears left. It is important to be able to cry alone because it allows you to thoroughly examine your feelings in a way that you can't when you're trying to keep it together in front of others, particularly your children. While you can honestly share your sadness with others, don't embroil others (especially your children) in the drama of your grief. If you're in therapy, you may wish to share this with your therapist in addition to mourning on your own. Be sure you are crying for your loss, not to get attention, sympathy, or evade personal responsibility for your life because you are so sad.

Personal responsibility is the key. Own your grief. No one "made you feel this way." It is just a very sad fact that your marriage is ending. More than half of marriages end in divorce. It *is* horrible, and so it's okay to feel horrible about it. Let yourself mourn this for you and everyone else who will ever get divorced in their lives.

By actually feeling your grief, and other painful emotions sooner rather than later, you may hurt intensely for a while but you'll actually get past those feelings faster than if you tried to hide them from yourself and not deal with them. As you work through this, understand that the journey from feeling bad to feeling okay is not linear and you may sometimes actually feel worse today than you did yesterday, and that is normal and natural. Your healing process is under way.

What Am I Sad About? Nancy's Story

Nancy was married to Alex, whom she had known since childhood. They grew up in the same neighborhood and went to school together from third grade through high school. When they divorced after only four years of marriage, Nancy was very, very sad. Sometimes she was so overwhelmed with grief that she didn't want to get out of bed in the morning. Worried that she would never feel good again, she decided to really get in touch with her sadness so she could work through it. She read the prompts in the next section to probe within and learn about her grief. Then she wrote about it in the following entry in her notebook:

I am so sad that my spouse is no longer my best friend. For a while, we really had it all. I never thought this would happen. Even though this hurts a lot, I need to grieve and I think this is just part of the process. I don't think that I'm letting my sadness help me avoid moving on or to avoid something else. I think it's real.

I think it is natural and healthy for me to be sad at this point.

I can make this easier if I take good care of myself. I can be sad but also keep up my exercise routine and make sure my eating habits support feeling good. I can reach out to my friends and suggest we do things that will help take my mind off the situation.

In addition to my friends, I will look for a divorce support group online. I will also talk to my aunt who lost her husband last year. She seemed to work through her sadness in a positive way and so maybe she has some suggestions.

This is a new feeling for me. I'm justified in missing my husband, but if I'm still feeling this way in three months then I will talk to a professional about it. I'm not really ready to let go of this yet. It will take time. While it's tempting just to go out to a bar and drink and flirt, I think that the real answer is that it will just take time.

I can keep a positive attitude and focus on my strengths. I am healthy and I am doing well at work. There are a lot of good things going right in my life so I will remember to do my gratitude exercise every day. I'm a strong person and I will get through this. I will keep reminding myself of that.

I have a couple of friends who got divorced in the last five years. If I can't figure this out on my own, and if the things I've outlined above don't work, I'll ask them.

If this were happening to my best friend I would say that recovering from a loss like this takes time, and to be gentle with herself. I would say that it's better to really feel these feelings and not to rush the recovery, because once you're done grieving your divorce you really want to be done. By pretending you're not sad, you risk never really healing. So it's okay to be sad. I would also be clear that if things weren't getting better in a few months that maybe she ought to talk to someone about it.

What Am I Sad About? Your Story

When you are feeling sad, the only way out is through. By allowing yourself to feel sad without trying to numb yourself, you will find that your sadness gives way to acceptance. The longer you put off feeling it, the longer it will take to get over. Use the questions below to prompt you to think about your sadness and then write about it in your notebook.

- What need does being sad serve for me?

- Is this natural, healthy sadness? Or am I letting it take over my life?

- Is there anything I can do to make this situation better?

- Is there somewhere I can go for support to help me be less sad about this?

- Is this recurring sadness that never gets resolved or addressed?

- If so, what can I do to stop that dynamic?

- What would it take for me to let go of this sadness?

- What can I do to help myself feel better?

- If I don't have any ideas about what to do, who can I turn to who can help me with this?

- If my best friend told me that he or she was sad about the same thing, what advice would I offer?

ACCEPTANCE

Acceptance is the final stage of the grieving process. People often confuse acceptance with the idea that what happened is okay and that you will feel happy about the loss of your marriage. That might be true for you. However, acceptance really has to do with understanding that your divorce is a reality and your life isn't going to be the same as it was when you were married. It can take a good deal of inner work to move toward accepting not just your divorce, but everything that occurred leading up to it. In the next chapter, you will learn how to move through this final stage of the grieving process.

CHAPTER 9

Forgiveness and Acceptance

Outside ideas of right doing and wrong doing there is a
field. I'll meet you there.

—RUMI

Holding a grudge is like drinking poison and waiting for the other
person to die. Holding on to anger, hurt, or sadness based on others'
past actions, thoughts, and comments has a corrosive effect on you. So
being unwilling or unable to forgive and move on hurts you, not the
other person. Forgiveness is a gift you give yourself, not someone else.

Acceptance is the last of the five stages of grief. It symbolizes that
you've processed the loss and are ready to look at the future and less
to the past. It's not that you're glad about the loss, but that you're not
stuck in it forever. Forgiveness and acceptance are natural comple-
ments: forgiveness helps us move to acceptance, and vice versa.

One of the biggest stressors you can inflict upon yourself is hanging on to anger long after the incident that aroused it. Anger expressed
constructively at the time it is felt can help you set good boundaries.
However, holding a grudge against someone for something they did
in the past that you have not resolved taxes your entire being.

Forgiveness can be a lightning rod topic for so many people. "He doesn't deserve my apology!" or "I've done nothing wrong so I'm not asking her to forgive me for anything!" But it's not about them. It's about what holding on to these negative thoughts is doing to *you*.

All too often the offense happened so long ago that everything else from that time is forgotten. Yet this issue still nags at you, and still makes you upset. The offender may have even forgotten that it happened at all. At this point it's no longer about whatever happened, it's about the time it takes up in your life, and the space it takes up in your head. It's taken on a life of its own. That's when you know it's really time to accept and forgive.

It doesn't matter what you call it. Whether you choose to call it forgiveness, letting it go, apology, moving on, refusing to bear a grudge, there's no need to get caught up in the label. For forgiveness to work, you have to find a way you can open a door in a dispute, even just a tiny bit, to see what happens, without feeling any sense of loss or compromise of your personal values. We call this practical forgiveness.

Practical forgiveness is *for you* and not the other person. It's difficult to believe this until you experience it personally, so we encourage you to prove it to yourself. We're going to help you figure out how to do that. We are most hurt by the people closest to us, so forgiveness is entirely practical because you'll use it in daily life and you'll get plenty of chances to practice.

The Meaning of Forgiveness

Some people are reluctant to "forgive" based on a misunderstanding of what forgiveness is. The way you're going to practice it is completely neutral and natural, free of any "shoulds." Forgiveness is entirely personal and will come in time, when you embrace the concept and its benefits and you're ready to try.

Practical forgiveness does *not* mean that:

- You weren't hurt or shouldn't have been hurt.

- What happened was okay.

- You must have a relationship with the person who hurt you (except in the case of divorcing spouses who want to effectively co-parent).

- You should forget, deny, or ignore what happened.

- You have to excuse the other person.

- You can feel morally superior and condemning toward the person you forgive.

- You can demand an apology or reparation.

- All your painful feelings are resolved at once.

- You must go along to get along, even if it means being abused.

- You will go back to the way things were before.

Making forgiveness a natural part of your relationship will make it easier to practice. People forgive more readily when they are not pressured to try hard. All you can expect of yourself or anyone else on any given day is to try your best to let go of resentment. As a result, you're able to relax into it and it begins to come naturally.

The Blame Game

When you get caught in the blame game, you get stuck and you can't forgive. The problem with this is that although you may be right and the other person is wrong, as you dwell on this trespass, it's taking up space in your brain. It's present in your thoughts and continues to make you upset even though the incident is long past. You're continuing to be "punished," yet you did nothing wrong. This is why learning to forgive is so important and why it's something you do for yourself, not someone else.

Holding on to blame echoes the same issues as not being willing to forgive. When we are hurting, the last place we look for the source of our pain is within. On some level, it just does not compute that we would purposely injure ourselves.

We immediately look to the environment to seek revenge for how bad we feel. Shifting blame feels terrific. We are absolved of any responsibility for our own upset and get all kinds of attention from compassionate friends when we vent and grouse. Blame has the same counterproductive, corrosive issues as refusing to forgive.

If you have held on to a grudge for longer than a month, you may already realize that it doesn't feel very good after all. Grudge holding has many druglike qualities. It feels good to wallow in self-righteousness, smug that you're right and the other person is wrong. After a while you find the buzz has worn off but you're addicted. You can't let go of this wrong that's been done to you. Who cares if your complaint is even true at this point? Holding on to this negativity is eating you alive.

When you blame someone else for the way you feel, you may feel unable to move on unless you get something from that person: apologizing, begging for forgiveness, admitting wrongdoing, or promising to treat you better. This takes you entirely out of the driver's seat and plunges you into a victim mentality. It leaves you at the mercy of someone else's decision to act in the way you've prescribed, and then you're wronged once again if the other person doesn't. Did you really mean to put all that power in someone else's hands?

Who Does Forgiveness Benefit?

Forgiveness is a paradox. We are accustomed to thinking that when we give something to someone else, they gain and we give something up. When you forgive someone else, *it benefits you.* This is entirely illogical to our human sense of giving. Only experience will show you this is true. Forgiving will not make you a better person; *you already are a good person.* Forgiving will make your life easier.

Don't forgive to manipulate an outcome. Forgive to release yourself from the prison of the past. You may hope that through forgiveness certain things will occur, yet this is not the same as demanding something you do not have the power to make happen.

Understanding the value of forgiveness every day in ways big and small will eventually lead you to forgive others and ask for forgiveness when you've made a mistake. You will more graciously accept imperfection in yourself and others. As long as you're still trying to do the right thing, you'll keep moving forward.

Practical Forgiveness: Julie and David's Story

Julie and David were married for four years and are now divorcing. Forgiving past hurts and old patterns is helping them move on and make their divorce work. Things between them are far from perfect, but there is far less acrimony than there would be if they weren't able to move through their anger and toward acceptance.

Several years before Julie and David found themselves heading toward divorce, Julie had an accident and totaled the family car. When the insurance check came, she spent the money, then borrowed to buy a new car instead of paying cash. David co-signed the loan reluctantly, but he saw this incident as just one of many concerning Julie's irresponsibility with money. Her spending habits were the subject of most of their fights. Then, in the midst of the divorce, when his application for a loan to buy a condo was denied because of the loan he co-signed for Julie's car, David discovered that Julie had fallen behind on the car payments.

David blew up at Julie: "You were always so irresponsible with money we could never get ahead! If you'd only taken my advice and paid cash for that car, we wouldn't be in this position. I'm still holding the bag for your mistakes."

Now David and Julie only communicate through lawyers.

After seeing his lawyer's bills, David realized that it was not only disheartening to be still fighting with Julie, it was also expensive . . . more expensive than her car payment. In his heart, David knew that Julie had always been a spendthrift. At first, her freewheeling money style was exciting to him, because he'd always been so conservative. The little presents she gave him, going to movies and fancy restaurants, were so romantic. In reality, he'd known all along that she spent more than they could afford. The condo situation was inconvenient, but cutting off communication wasn't going to suddenly make Julie into a financially responsible person.

David decided to apologize. "I am sorry that it's come to this. I wish you could have told me you were having trouble with the car payment. I wouldn't have been happy, but we could've figured something out before it also screwed up my condo deal." Amazed that David apologized to her when she'd caused the initial problem, Julie replied, "I'm sorry I hid that from you. I really thought I could catch up on the payments. But then again, I always think that and I'm usually wrong. Is there anything I can do to help?"

Forgiveness does not necessarily have anything to do with ideas of morality, goodness, religion, or spirituality. It can if you want it to, but it doesn't have to have those connotations. Your focus is on letting go of resentment in a way that makes sense to you. Forgiveness comes in small steps when you identify little ways you can loosen the grip of a conflict without feeling pressured or rushing into an inauthentic, shallow apology. Or it may come after a long, negative conversation, when one person has a sudden flash of compassion or the realization of how fruitless it is to hold on to something that happened long ago.

Some days will be easier than others, and "your best" will fluctuate depending on the level of responsibility you are willing to accept, your ability to resist the temptation to blame, and the stresses in life that can seem to thwart the best of intentions.

You do not have to forget anything that happened to you, but you do want to let go of the pain associated with the memory. You can integrate what you need to learn from the situation and set good boundaries, yet not be crippled every time you think of what happened.

Forgiving Yourself: Dylan's Story

Dylan was married to Kate for eight years before they divorced. Though both Dylan and Kate turned outside their marriage and it eroded over time, Dylan felt especially bad that he had an emotional affair with another woman. He had a tremendous amount of guilt over his indiscretion, and he was beating himself up rather than allowing himself to move on with his life. Kate told him she forgave him, but that wasn't enough. He knew he needed to forgive himself, but he wasn't sure how to do it. He read through the questions in the next section to examine how he hurt Kate and how he could forgive himself and move on. He wrote the following entry in his notebook about the hurt he caused and how he could move past his mistakes:

I made a mistake and hurt my wife when I started an emotionally intimate relationship with a female coworker three years ago. When my wife found out, I said, "We didn't sleep together!" but I knew that this relationship was much too close to be appropriate for a married man and another woman. When I did this, I was feeling so lost in my marriage, so unappreciated. I felt like no one understood me like this other woman. I felt like my wife was shutting me out. Instead of turning to my wife, I turned to someone else. That was a big mistake. I knew that my wife would be livid if she knew about my new relationship at work. When she found out she was beside herself. It shook the foundations of our relationship and I don't think she ever trusted me again.

Now that we're getting divorced, I'm still disappointed in myself that I didn't address the deep freeze I felt with my wife. If we had talked about how I felt at the time, maybe we would have been able to fix our relationship. Instead, my emotional affair just hastened the end of our marriage. We're getting divorced and it feels like it's my fault. If I had it to do over again I would've approached my wife, not some stranger, with my problems.

If I ever find myself in this kind of a situation again, I will try my best to be honest about my feelings instead of sneaking around. I hope that I can prove to my ex that I am trustworthy by being honest with her right away, as soon as a problem arises. We have some joint credit card debt and a house to sell and some hard financial decisions to make. I am going to be forthright with her in these transactions.

When things were great between us, I saw her as the most trusting, kind person I'd ever met. I saw how she really brought out the best in me and how happy we were. I don't know why I turned into a secretive person, and why I stopped turning to her with my needs and problems, but I'm not going to let that happen again.

Forgiving Yourself: Your Story

Writing your own story will help you identify those areas in which you need to forgive yourself. You may find yourself coming back to this section when different issues arise about which you may be feeling guilty. The following prompts will guide you to be as fully expressive about each issue as possible. No one will read these stories but you, so don't feel that there's anything too childish and self-centered to write down. In fact, the more you accept even the most trivial-seeming feelings, the better you will understand yourself and accept your own imperfections.

Some things to consider about accepting and moving past your mistakes are listed below. Use them to write up your story about how you can forgive yourself. If you don't want to write a whole story, just jot down some notes.

I made a mistake and hurt (the person).

What I did that hurt (the person) is (what you did).

What I said that hurt (the person) is (what you said).

When I hurt (the person) I was feeling (what you felt).

I believe that I hurt (the person) because (he or she) angered or disappointed me in the following ways (what you think the person "did to you" that prompted you to hurt them).

The consequences of my hurtful words and actions are that (how the person was hurt by you).

Now that the hurtful event has passed, I feel (what you feel now).

The ways that my relationship is now damaged with (the person) include (the damage you did).

If I had it to do over again, I would (what would you do).

Next time something like this happens between me and (the person), I will try my best to (what will you do next time instead).

I hope (what you hope will happen between you).

When things were the best they ever were between me and (the person), I saw (him or her) as (how you saw the person in his or her best light).

When things were the best they ever were between me and (the person), I saw myself in relationship to (the person) as (how you saw yourself when things were good) between you and (the person).

Forgiving Yourself: Exercise

Here is an exercise you can do to accelerate your experience of forgiving yourself. Copy the paragraph below verbatim on a piece of paper separate from your notebook, filling in your name, the name of the person you hurt, and a very brief name for the incident. It is not necessary to go into detail about what happened because you are going to let it go.

When you feel ready, do the breathing exercise for a few minutes, until you feel relaxed. Then read the paragraph either out loud or to yourself, whichever feels right.

I (your name) regret hurting (the person) by (a very brief name for the incident). I know I am human and simply made a mistake that I want to correct now. I have a deep desire to put this in the past and learn from my mistake. I understand that forgiving myself will bring me to the peace I need to make sure something like this doesn't happen again. I choose to forgive myself whether I feel like I deserve it or not, knowing that forgiveness is not based on merit, rather it is something I can freely give to and accept for myself. My forgiveness is for me and me alone. I allow myself this gift and the liberty it grants me now to live a life free of the pain my nonforgiveness toward myself has caused me.

When you are finished, shred or burn your paper. If you want to come back to this issue again and again, you may do so. It is important, however, that you start fresh and rewrite the statement each time. Re-reading what you wrote in an earlier exercise is not necessary, nor is it helpful to hold on to your statements to check to see if you are making progress. Your progress is measured in the amount of peace you feel within yourself and in your interactions with the person you hurt.

Forgiving Another Person: Tammy's Story

Tammy was married to George for seventeen years and they had five children. George traveled a lot for work, which frustrated Tammy and led to a lot of disappointment in their marriage. Tammy was so angry at George for leaving her alone each and every week that when he came home on the weekends, all they did was argue about how much he was gone. Then she learned that George had been carrying on an emotionally intimate relationship with another woman. Even though Tammy blamed George for most of their problems, she knew that if she didn't forgive him, it would eat her up inside and make her bitter.

Tammy read the prompts in the next section and got in touch with how she could open herself to forgiving George for her own sake. It took some time. She wasn't ready to do it right away. She forgave him in little bits that culminated in her eventually letting go and accepting what she had before seen as something George "did to her." The following is an entry from her notebook:

It was so hard raising five kids mostly without George's help. Then he started up with his "emotional friend" and that really put me over the edge. He says that it was just talking and no sex, but I don't really care because he was obviously in love with her. When I learned of this relationship, I felt horribly betrayed. I also felt very foolish. How could I not have noticed? The result was that I lost all trust in my husband.

In retrospect, I believe that he may have hurt me because this was during a rough patch in our marriage and we weren't speaking much. Looking back, all we did was argue. Now that he's ended that relationship and we're getting divorced, I still feel let down and disappointed, and our relationship is irreparably damaged.

I forgive him and I'm going to tell him, "I'm sorry I was so judgmental and nagging toward you at the end of our relationship. No wonder you started talking to someone else instead of me. When things were good between us, I always appreciated how supportive you were of me and I'm sorry we had to lose that part of our relationship."

Forgiving Another Person: Your Story

Choose a grudge you are holding that you feel you are ready to loosen your grip on. You may not feel entirely ready to let go, and that is okay. You may have to come back to this exercise several times before you find you are completely free of resentment. Usually, whatever issue comes to mind first is the one you subconsciously want to work on, even if it feels scary and insurmountable. The person you resent (or even hate) will never see this worksheet, so be sure to express all your anger, even if it feels scary. The scared feeling is the rancor being stirred up within you and coming to the surface of your emotions to be released.

Contemplate the prompts below and write your thoughts and feelings about the situation in your notebook.

(The person) made a mistake and hurt me.

What (the person) did that hurt me is (what he or she did).

What (the person) said that hurt me is (what he or she said).

When (the person) hurt me I felt (what you felt).

I believe (the person) may have hurt me because I angered or disappointed (the person) in the following ways (what you think you may have "done to" the person that prompted him or her to hurt you).

The consequences of (the person's) hurtful words and actions are that (how you were hurt by the person).

Now that the hurtful event has passed, I feel (what you feel now).

The ways that my relationship is now damaged with (the person) include (the damage the person did).

If I had it to do over again, I would (what would you do).

Next time something like this happens between me and (the person), I will try my best to (what will you do next time instead).

I hope (what you hope will happen between you).

When things were the best they ever were between me and (the person), I saw (him or her) as (how you saw the person in his or her best light).

When things were the best they ever were between me and (the person), I saw myself in relationship to (the person) as (how you saw yourself when things were good) between you and (the person).

Forgiving Another Person: Exercise

This exercise is just like the exercise for forgiving yourself, only you direct it toward someone you would like to forgive, to free yourself from holding on to your grudge. On a piece of paper separate from your notebook, copy the statement below exactly as it is written. Fill in the words in parentheses to fit your situation. When you feel ready, relax by using the breathing exercise and then read the statement out loud or in the privacy of your own mind.

I (your name) feel hurt by (the person) because (he or she) (a very brief name for the incident). I know (the person) is human and simply made a mistake. We all make mistakes. I have a deep desire to put this in the past and move into the now, free of pain. I understand that forgiving (the person) will bring me to the peace I need to think clearly and rebuild my life. I choose to forgive (the person) whether I feel like (he or she) deserves it or not, knowing that forgiveness is not based on merit, rather it is something I can freely extend to (the person). My forgiveness is for me and me alone. I allow myself this gift and the liberty it grants me now to live a life free of the pain my non-forgiveness toward (the person) has caused me. I am not saying I was not hurt and I am not saying (the person) was right. I am simply accepting peace in this moment.

When you are finished, shred or burn your paper. Do the exercise as many times as you need to, until you feel at peace with the person you are seeking to forgive.

Learning to forgive takes practice. Getting to the acceptance stage of grieving the loss of your marriage takes patience. As you learn to let go of the things that cause you pain, you'll find that your life becomes much more balanced. Staying mired in your grief, holding on to grudges, losing friendships, and scorekeeping make you a difficult person to be around. When you're willing to forgive, and accept that others are human, with all of their faults, you create opportunities for kindness and generosity.

GRATITUDE EXERCISE

Gratitude and forgiveness go hand in hand. When you are grateful, you tend to be more forgiving and accepting. Human beings are hardwired to look for danger, and as a result we often focus more on the negatives than the positives. By practicing this gratitude exercise you can reroute that negative hard wiring and cultivate an increasingly optimistic attitude that supports this new chapter in your life. Now that you've grieved the loss of your marriage in a healthy and constructive way and learned to forgive, you can celebrate the little (and big) things that make life worth living.

Think of ten things you are thankful for. Write them down. If you can only think of five, then start with five. If you can think of twenty, then write all twenty down. The things you're thankful for can be very small. They can also change every day.

Do this every day. Do it more than once a day if you think of it.

Over time, you will become a more optimistic person because you'll continually focus on what's positive in your life instead of dwelling only on what's negative.

This is a simple exercise, but it works.

SAMPLE GRATITUDE EXERCISE

I am thankful that:

- My dog loves me.
- My parents are healthy.
- The sweater I gave my friend for her birthday fit perfectly.
- I can walk to the grocery store.
- I shot an 80 at golf last week.
- My favorite team is playing on Saturday.
- I'm having coffee with a friend in two hours.
- Our son got a B on his spelling test and the last one was a C.
- It's a beautiful sunny day.
- I'm looking forward to sleeping in Saturday morning.

When you complete your own gratitude list, reflect on how different you feel from the way you felt before you wrote down the first item.

Making Your Divorce Work

You have now added practical forgiveness to your peacemaking skills. And you're ready to forgive because you've worked through all the stages of grief and loss in mourning the demise of your relationship. You now have a number of ways to deal with and resolve old (and new) disputes and to truly let them go and put them behind you. The emotional issues are mostly out of the way, although they'll always be a work in progress, and you've come to terms with how and why your marriage is ending. Coupled with everything you've already learned, you're ready to deal with the legal aspects of the divorce. As you can see, there was a lot of work to get ready to negotiate your settlement.

In the next chapter, you'll learn how to use everything that you've learned to this point to set and accomplish your financial, support, and parenting goals and negotiate a win-win legal settlement.

CHAPTER 10

Negotiating Your Settlement

You can't always get what you want. But if you try sometimes you might find you get what you need.

—THE ROLLING STONES

Now that you've set your personal goals and priorities for how
you'd like for your divorce to look when you're done, it's time to
think about actually handling the nuts and bolts of the divorce
itself. It doesn't matter if you're settling your divorce yourself
around the kitchen table, using a mediator, or going to court—
there are going to be plenty of opportunities to negotiate. This
chapter teaches you how.

This chapter will cover three key areas of concern:

• Understanding the three main sources of divorce disputes
  and how to address them

• How to decide what you want and need from your settlement

• How to negotiate your settlement

Three Main Sources of Divorce Disputes

Most divorce disputes aren't actually about the law. Once in a while a question of law comes into play, but most legal questions that arise have more to do with clarifying what the law actually says (information) rather than with interpretation and advice.

Most disagreements in divorce cases involve the value of assets and other issues around *facts*. The next most common type of dispute involves conflicts over *relationship* issues, such as communication problems. And sometimes there are geographic or *structural* conflicts, like a long-distance move away with children. As you can see, the three major areas of disputes don't involve looking anything up in a law book. That's good news for you.

FACT DISPUTES

Disagreements involving facts may turn out to be the easiest to tackle; you can pull together most of the information you will need on your own, with a little research. Don't know what all of your assets are, and what they are worth? Start by making a list of what you *do* know about and what you suspect is missing. Take a look at that pile of papers in the den, or the filing cabinet in the garage. Ask your spouse to help. This should not necessarily be a covert operation. Check the most recent bank statements. Ask a Realtor for an estimate of your house's value. Look on the Internet to find out how much your car is worth. A little legwork will give you more peace of mind.

Got a dispute over parenting time? Start with everyone's schedule. For most families, work, school, and extracurricular activities practically dictate most of the parenting schedule. At the very least, you can easily narrow down the times when both parents are available, which limits the scope of your dispute. Now, instead of all seven days, you're discussing the two and a half days a week when both of you would like to be with the children.

It may feel like we're being glib here, but honestly, most of the disputes we see in mediation are fact disputes. A couple of times a year we drag out the law books and look something up, but more often than not we're suggesting that clients speak with Realtors to find out how much their house is worth, look up car values online, and gather up credit card statements. Just the facts.

Even if you can't solve your fact dispute with the information you gather, you'll make progress toward resolution and you'll narrow down the scope of the issues. And if your case is headed to court, you'll need to put this information together for your lawyer anyway, so acting proactively now will also save money.

RELATIONSHIP CONFLICTS

Plenty of divorcing couples have relationship issues. By this we mean difficulties in how you communicate—from coolly civil to downright hostile, poor communication, noncommunication, frequent miscommunication, or engaging in repetitive negative behavior, couples may experience the full gamut of relationship conflicts in varying degrees. You're getting divorced, after all. And chances are many of these emotionally charged issues got you where you are today. As a practical matter, if you couldn't solve those issues in the marriage, you're probably not going to do so in your divorce, yet you can develop protocols and skills to get around the difficulties in communication.

First, figure out what causes communication to break down. If you can pinpoint the issues that trigger conflict, you can start to find ways to navigate around them. Does one co-parent like to stay in touch by calling several times a day, when the other co-parent would prefer an email every two days? Do discussions devolve into the same old fight, even if you started out by talking civilly? Does your spouse's tone of voice send you into a tailspin even if the topic is the weather?

You don't need to figure out why you have relationship conflicts in order to find a solution. You just need to be able to realize that you have these types of conflicts and then develop strategies to work around them in a very nuts-and-bolts way.

One of our most successful interventions in relationship conflicts is helping couples develop a communication hierarchy, since these conflicts almost always revolve around difficulties in communicating. Before you initiate communication, you ask yourself "How urgent is this?" The degree of urgency dictates the kind of communication you'll use. Do you honestly need an answer right this minute? Pick up the phone. Do you need an answer tomorrow? Use email or voicemail. And if it's just about notice, and you don't need an answer, use the least intrusive method of communication you can think of to deliver the information.

Relationship Conflicts: Ed's Story

Ed and Julie were struggling with communication issues. Julie would pick up the phone and call Ed about every little thing, and Ed began to dread seeing her caller ID pop up on his phone and just let her calls go to voicemail. Frustrated that she was never able to get ahold of Ed, Julie started calling more frequently. We worked with Julie and Ed to come up with a communication hierarchy.

Julie and Ed chose to use an online parenting calendar. Their ten-year-old daughter, Olivia, helped them to keep it updated for long lead issues, like her soccer schedule and school functions. When Olivia got a sleepover invitation, she added it to the calendar and Julie sent an email to Ed to let him know, since the date was on his parenting time, so it was his responsibility to RSVP.

For twenty-four-hour turnaround events, Ed and Julie agreed to send an email or text message. For same-day issues and emergencies, they decided to use the phone.

Now when Ed sees Julie's caller ID on his phone, he picks up immediately. Because Julie knows that Ed checks his email regularly, she isn't afraid that her messages aren't getting through and no longer needs to use the phone every time she wants to let Ed know about something. Now that their communication follows the hierarchy, they have less day-to-day contact and that helps them keep the conflict down.

The same structure can be used for a couple without children who have difficulty communicating but who need to sell their house. For next week's handyman appointment, use a shared online calendar or email. For the painter whose schedule suddenly freed up, send an email or text message, since the painter is coming tomorrow. When the Realtor calls and says there's a showing in an hour, use the telephone.

Remember, the key here is that you're not going to fix anything. You're going to work around it. If your spouse tries to pick a fight every time you talk, you're not going to be able to stop that behavior—and neither is a court. But if your main form of communication is now email, and not the telephone, your spouse probably won't want those harsh words in writing and you can avoid taking the bait. Relationship conflicts are one of the main reasons court cases get to be so expensive and needlessly complicated, mainly because they're problems the court can't fix. A court can order your spouse to stop making snide comments to you on the phone, but that same court won't want to hear a contempt motion for a violation of that order, and that's not a good use of your fee dollars either. Making an honest effort to find ways to work around relationship conflicts will make your settlement discussions and post-divorce life much more peaceful.

STRUCTURAL CONFLICTS

Structural conflicts occur when there is literally something in the way of resolving your settlement. The two most common examples both involve living arrangements: a move by one partner, especially with children, and the disposition of a house, if neither spouse can comfortably afford to purchase from the other.

The key to settling structural conflicts is not unlike resolving most conflicts: figuring out different ways to deal with the obstacle. That is, looking for options. If it's a move away, would it make sense for the other parent to move, too? Or how will the children travel back and forth? And is the move essential? If it's not, would there be a way to avoid having to move, like providing more support in exchange for turning down a promotion in another city? For the house situation, is there a place other than the bank to get the money needed to buy out the house? Should the house be sold? Or can you live with owning the house together for a period of time and then reevaluating what to do? For structural conflicts, it's all about generating options and then choosing the most reasonable solution.

When structural conflicts are left to a court to decide, often there's one winner and one loser. Either the child moves, or he doesn't. Either one of you buys the house, or it's sold. The judge will make a decision, and you have a 50/50 shot that it will go your way. And even if the judge does rule in your favor, it may not be on your terms—for example, you're permitted to move with your children but have to pay for all of their transportation back and forth, or you can buy the house but only if you pay your spouse immediately, otherwise it must be sold. By being prepared to come up with creative options to resolve structural conflicts, you'll be able to stay in control of the outcome of your case while also thinking constructively about how to create a solution.

No matter what the nature of your disputes, if you break each down into manageable pieces and determine what options you have available, before you know it, you'll have an agreement. And even if you're working with a mediator or lawyer to help settle your case, by understanding the type of dispute and how to address it, you're going to be a much more active partner in the resolution of your case. This will save you money and time as well as insure that your final agreement is tailored to your individual situation.

How to Decide What You Want— and Need—from Your Settlement: Cathy's Dilemma

As part of her divorce settlement, Cathy was determined that she'd keep the house. In fact, she became almost obsessive about it, to the exclusion of other issues. But she never really thought that in order to keep the house she might have to give up other things to which she felt she had a legitimate right. This house was in a great neighborhood with a good school system. But, more to the point, it was what she had thought would be her dream home . . . She had a lot emotionally invested in this place.

The reality was, however, that she didn't know if she could afford the home on her own since technically she'd have to buy her husband out and then be solely responsible for whatever mortgage was outstanding, the taxes, and the upkeep. Child support couldn't be stretched to cover the shortfall.

She dreaded the idea of moving but was equally anxious that a judgment wouldn't go in her favor and allow her to keep the house. She was stuck in a place where she found it difficult to separate her wants from her needs, and she was finding it increasingly difficult to see the options.

Whether you're negotiating on your own or working with a

mediator or lawyer, you're going to determine what you want and how important each request is.

- What do you want from your property settlement, support settlement, and parenting plan?

- Can you distinguish between your wants and needs—and set priorities for dealing with them?

- Can you figure out *why* you want what you want, and what underlying interest it meets?

- Can you evaluate whether your goals are realistic?

- Are you able to look at your requests from your spouse's perspective?

- Can you expand your settlement options based on your needs and interests, not just your statement about what you want?

Cathy wondered whether trying to keep the house was worth the other sacrifices she'd have to make and, looking at the big picture, asked herself what she could accomplish in her settlement that would meet the same need as keeping the house. After all, she finally admitted, a house is really just a place to live. As much as she might be attached to it, she recalled how attached she was to her first apartment, too. So she started to look for options: if they sold the house or she accepted a buyout from her husband, was there a smaller house or condo in the same neighborhood that would also be a nice place to live and in which she could create new memories?

By not getting stuck in just one position, such as "I want to keep the house," Cathy started to open up the range of possible settlements rather than just getting stuck on simply what she wanted.

Settlement Goals: Vicki's Story

Vicki's top three financial priorities in her divorce settlement are: she wants to keep the house, she wants to keep her teachers' pension intact, and she wants to keep the wedding gifts. She wants the house because it has sentimental value and it's in a good school district and the children won't have to change schools. Her teachers' pension will insure she can retire as planned, and she wants the wedding gifts because she's the only one who cares about the china and most of the gifts came from her family anyway. She figures that her husband, Bill, has already figured out that she wants the house, her pension, and the gifts and that it won't be a huge surprise to him, although she knows he'd like to live in the house, too. She anticipates that he may want to buy her out of the house as one of his top priorities, along with keeping his IRA and 401(k) and making sure that he gets his grandmother's silverware back even though Vicki considers it to be a wedding gift. She also assumes he'll want his car, the boat, and all of his expensive tools. She knows that retiring is important to Bill, too, and that he's done so many DIY projects around the house that he probably feels like it should be his.

Now that she's articulated what it is that she wants, and why, and she's also thought through what Bill will probably want, Vicki is feeling less nervous about the settlement. The house feels like the only possible big issue. Vicki hopes that Bill's 401(k) and IRA will be equal trade-offs with her pension, or that Bill won't care if there's a little difference in value. Considering the silverware, Vicki figures that she'd probably feel the same way Bill feels about it if it had belonged to Vicki's grandmother, so she's prepared to give Bill the silver if the rest of the wedding gifts can be hers. And Vicki doesn't want the boat or the tools. As it turns out, there are a number of requests Vicki anticipates from Bill that will be easy to give in on, or make a fair trade for something else.

The other things on the list—the time-share, the frequent flier miles, the college football season tickets, and the credit cards—Vicki thinks will be easy to settle, either by dividing them 50/50 or trading one for the other.

Vicki's questions all involve the house: What's the value? How much would she need to pay Bill to buy him out? Where can she get the money? Would she qualify for a loan from a bank or can her family lend her the money? Before Vicki approaches Bill about buying the house from him, she does a little investigation, calling a Realtor, a bank, a mortgage broker, and her brother. She finds out what the house is worth, how much she'll need to borrow, and that she's eligible to be approved for the loan. Now Vicki knows she can indeed afford to buy the house from Bill.

But Vicki knows Bill feels strongly about the house, too. Given what she found out about the house value and financing, he can probably afford to buy her out also. Instead of bracing herself for a fight, Vicki starts to think about what will happen if she and Bill don't have an agreement. A judge might order the house sold. Going to court is expensive. It would also be stressful and take several months. The impact of all of this on Vicki's overall settlement would be huge, especially if she has to pay a lawyer and take time off work.

Vicki starts to think about choices. One option would be to pay Bill a premium for the house, maybe 5 percent over value, which might entice him to take her offer. Or maybe Bill would offer her the same deal, so Vicki asks the Realtor about other available properties in the neighborhood just in case. Vicki starts to think about what it would be like to live somewhere else. She's not thrilled, but she doesn't rule it out, either. Vicki decides that she'll ask Bill about it at their next private discussion so that she can get an idea of how important the house is to him and whether this is really an issue, and what it might take to settle this issue.

YOUR SETTLEMENT

A remarkable number of people file for divorce, hire a lawyer, and go to court without ever really thinking through what they want out of the process. With the ideas and guidance you've gleaned so far in this book, and with the goal setting exercise that follows, you will be more than prepared to decide what your goals and priorities are for your divorce settlement. Going through this exercise—before you talk to your spouse or a lawyer—will save you time, money, and heartache.

The vision plan you completed in chapter 6 is the foundation for this next phase of goal setting. Your vision plan sets your course for your overarching goals for the divorce—who and how you want to be when you finish. This next goal setting exercise deals with the details of your settlement, including the details of your property settlement, support, and parenting plan.

As you work your way through this exercise, get help if you need it. Sensible relatives and friends can be a good sounding board. But choose to confide in someone who will be more than just a cheerleader and who won't derail all your hard work by saying that you deserve *everything*. You need a reality check. And since most divorce decisions are financial rather than actual legal disputes, consider seeing an accountant, financial planner, or certified divorce financial analyst instead of or in addition to a lawyer. We know everyone thinks that the legal aspects of his or her case are unique and that a top lawyer is needed to get the best deal. In reality, this probably isn't true. Very few divorce cases involve complicated *legal* disputes. Most divorces involve disputes concerning facts, relationship issues, or structural conflicts.

Earlier in this book you looked at the issue of knowing why you want what you want. The answer to this question will enable you to figure out different ways to get what you need in a much more concrete way as you translate your earlier vision plan and mission statement into your actual divorce settlement.

Lastly, remember that you are not alone in this process. If you want to have an agreement, it will have to be one that your spouse will sign. It's critical that you understand your spouse's goals and priorities in the settlement. So pretending that your spouse's needs are not important or that you don't care is counterproductive. They are important and you do need to care, even if it's only for your own self-interest. Ask yourself "What will have to be in the agreement in order for my spouse to sign it?"

Goal Setting for Your Settlement

The following checklist can serve as a reminder of the common divorce issues. While this list may be long and seem somewhat daunting, it is important that you address all the pertinent issues up front and determine what are the important ones to you—and to your spouse. Inevitably, your list will be shorter than this one; it will reflect the things that are of most concern to you.

- Parenting plan, interim parenting plan
  - Decision making
  - Day-to-day schedule
  - Vacations, holidays, and travel
  - Other parenting issues, like house rules

- Child support
  - Monthly amount
  - Add-on expenses, like work-related child care, sports, lessons, camp, etc.
  - College and post–high school education (optional, since your children will technically be adults by then)

- Spousal support, alimony, maintenance, and/or spousal support buyout
- Interim support and interim financial arrangements
- Move-out expenses
- House, mortgages
- Apartment or rental home, occupancy of apartment, security deposit
- Other real estate, like rental properties, apartment buildings
- Bank accounts
- Retirement assets—for example, 401(k) plan, IRA, pension, profit sharing plans
- Savings, investments, stocks, mutual funds (non-retirement)
- Cars, RVs, other vehicles
- Frequent flier miles
- Insurance: health insurance, car insurance, life insurance
- Personal property, pets
- Debts: student loans, personal loans, loans from family
- Filing taxes for the current year, back taxes, tax loss carry forward
- Business(es)
- Claims on property you brought into the marriage or inherited, reimbursement claims
- Intellectual property: patents, trademarks, copyrights, songs, books, scripts, works in progress

- Stock options

- Privately held investments, limited partnerships

- Season tickets, country club memberships

- Frozen embryos, eggs, or sperm

- Injury settlements and lawsuits, workers compensation, car accidents

- Time-share(s)

- Mediation fees, attorneys' fees, financial advisor fees, other professional fees

Now get out your notebook and follow the prompts and questions below to outline your goals and to start thinking strategically about your settlement discussion. Write everything out. You'll be glad you have detailed notes when you're discussing this with your spouse, lawyer, or mediator, particularly if you're nervous.

You will probably already have eliminated those issues that are not pertinent to your case, which immediately makes this list more manageable. You will begin by determining your top three priorities in each of the following areas: your parenting plan, support settlement, and property settlement. You will complete three of these worksheets in your notebook, one for each area:

- My top three priorities for my parenting plan/support settlement/property settlement:
  - These are my priorities because:

- My spouse's reaction to hearing what I want with regard to these topics will be:
  - Because:

- I anticipate that my spouse will want:
  - Because:

- My reaction to those requests is:
  - Because:

- The three things I can most easily give up are:

- The questions I have are:

- Do I need more information before I can make a decision? What kind of information? Here's my list:

- What parts of my spouse's requests will I be able to honor without compromising on what means most to me?

- If we don't have an agreement, my alternatives are:

- The cost of these alternatives would be:
  - Financial:
  - Emotional:
  - Time:
  - Impact on children, family, and career:

- What are my choices if we can't resolve our divorce on our own?

NEGOTIATING YOUR SETTLEMENT

Negotiating should not be about getting the biggest slice of the pie—it's about learning to make the pie bigger. And the key to resolving your differences and reaching a settlement is expanding your options through a mediation technique called *interest-based negotiation*.

Interest-based negotiations spring from the goals that you have determined for yourself. For example, if part of your vision plan is to remain a meaningful part of your children's school life as well as weekend life, or to be able to have financial security after the divorce, those are your overarching goals. But there may be several different ways to meet these goals in the details of your settlement.

During a divorce, many people become very *position-based*, articulating a settlement proposal in absolute terms ("I want 100 percent of the 401(k)") and losing sight of the *interest-based* goal (to be financially secure) that they hope these positions will achieve.

You should always be looking for options. When you expand the position "I want 100 percent of the 401(k)" to "I want to be able to retire like I've planned to and not worry about money," there may be several ways to secure those retirement goals, and they may or may not have to do with controlling 100 percent of the 401(k).

EXPANDING THE OPTIONS

The first step in the negotiating process is to define your goals for the settlement, like we did in the second part of this chapter. Remember, these are your goals, not your positions. Framing everything in terms of goals gives everyone more bargaining room. It increases your options and makes the pie bigger.

Many people think that divorce negotiations are all about compromise. This is only partly true. A true win-win settlement occurs when both spouses accomplish their *most important goals* with the fewest compromises, and give way more on their less important goals. That is why it is so important for each person to set his or her priorities in order, to make sure the most important goals are accomplished.

Here's a sample of positions that can be articulated in terms of the underlying goal (interest):

Position	Interest
"I want Wednesday night overnights."	I want to be involved in parenting my child during school time as well as vacation time. I don't want to be stuck being a "Disneyland parent."
"I don't want to pay spousal support."	I want to be financially secure, and to be able to retire when I'm ready.
"You have to pay my college tuition."	I want to be able to support myself.
"That 401(k) is mine, and I'm not dividing it."	I want recognition for being the saver in the family, and I don't want to feel punished for trying to do the right thing.
"My business is mine, not yours."	I've poured my heart and soul into getting the business off the ground, and I don't want anything to jeopardize what I've built.

As you can see, for example, the goal of being an involved parent can be solved by something other than Wednesday night overnights. Maybe there are Tuesday night overnights, or Thursday, or maybe the parent can coach a sports team or volunteer at the school. It's not all about Wednesday nights.

POSITIONAL BARGAINING VS. INTEREST-BASED NEGOTIATION

Interest-based negotiation is a fundamental shift in thinking that lets go of the labels in favor of the underlying issues. When you get stuck in your position, you assume that resources are limited, that everyone is going to have to compromise, and that the glass will always be half-empty. You're convinced that your way is the only way, so your spouse should just accept your position. You'll probably get to an agreement eventually—most couples do—but it will be rough going.

When you focus on your interests, not your positions, the pie gets bigger as you start to think about nonmonetary solutions and value-added solutions.

For people with children, this might mean calling each other first to babysit before hiring a sitter if you can't be with the children during your parenting time. You save money and the other parent gets more time with the kids. Or you could agree that you'll both attend all the children's soccer games, so that you'll each get to see the kids on Saturday mornings. For couples without kids, it could mean that one spouse pays all of the debt in exchange for paying less alimony or spousal support, which relieves the other spouse from having to worry about the creditors and the tax burden of receiving spousal support.

The key is in your attitude. Ask yourself "What can I offer that works for me and is also valuable to the other person?"

Interest-based negotiations enlarge the range of alternatives so that the needs of all parties are addressed and met to the greatest extent possible. This is the basis of most mediation, but you don't have to be a professional to negotiate this way. It's mostly about knowing your heart, and your facts, and having a little empathy for the other person. After all, you need your spouse to sign the agreement, so it's going to have to work for both of you.

Interest-based negotiations work best when you can recognize your common interests and have a little bit of trust in each other. It helps if both people are on a relatively equal footing power-wise, so it is essential for you to identify your own strengths—and those of your spouse—going into the negotiations. It may be that one of you knows more about the finances and the other is mostly in charge of the children. In that instance, you each have power, although it's a different kind of power. Each of you has something to offer the other.

WHAT IF I DON'T KNOW WHAT MY SPOUSE'S SETTLEMENT GOALS ARE?

Understanding your own goals is only half of the equation. If your spouse hasn't thought much about the settlement or won't share those thoughts with you, then you're going to start by giving her the benefit of the doubt. Maybe your spouse hasn't done the goal setting worksheets in this book. She may not even know what her goals are. Or she may be so entrenched in her position that she doesn't even know what her interests are. She may not know that it's possible to think about her position in a different way and expand the array of options.

Your spouse may be hiding his interests thinking that this is some sort of strategy. The irony of this is that before going to court he's going to have to submit written proposals and all of his financial information. The court may even do an investigation into the finances or custody concerns. So this so-called "strategy" of secrecy is soon going to become a matter of public record.

But you're going to forgive your spouse for a lack of insight. You're going to say things like "Help me to understand why that is so important to you" and "If you got that, what goal would that accomplish for you? What need would it meet?"

Or maybe you're complaining, "Why do I always have to do everything in this relationship?" or "I am done taking care of my spouse, and that includes taking responsibility for all of negotiations." But you're doing this for you. It's gratifying to think that maybe you could also feel generous toward your spouse, who doesn't know about interest-based negotiations, and help to educate her, but it's not necessary. You're taking responsibility for guiding the discussion because you want to have an agreement that meets everyone's needs.

You're better off in the long run if your spouse is at least reasonably happy with the agreement, too. If you need cooperation in selling the house, do you want to work with a disgruntled co-seller who'd love to see you wait for your share of the proceeds, or a cooperative co-seller who wants the house sold as quickly as you do? And if you're co-parenting, then you really need each other's cooperation.

It's easy to fall into the trap of thinking that there's only one solution—or no solution—during the dark days of your divorce. But that's not true.

Best Intentions

In addition to understanding the three main kinds of conflicts in divorces, your own goals and priorities for the settlement, and how to negotiate in order to reach a settlement, you each need to *want* to settle and you have to *be ready* to settle. If you're ready to and want to get things settled, it will happen. If one or both people aren't ready to, or don't want to, resolve the issues, then you probably won't reach a resolution.

The need or desire to work together in the future, whether it's raising children or not making your mutual friends choose sides, is important because it helps to keep you at the negotiation table when you are tempted to give up. It's worth it to preserve what's left of your relationship. It's easier in the long run to be civil, if not outright friends, because when you hold grudges and cling to negativity in your life, it hurts you, not the person you're trying to punish. Remember, the plan is to have a decent, respectful divorce that will be a role model to your children, families, and friends.

TALKING WITH YOUR SPOUSE ABOUT A SETTLEMENT

Even if you're working with a professional to resolve your case, as much as you may hope that your lawyer or mediator will do all of this work for you, you and your spouse are probably going to have lots of discussions outside of court or mediation sessions—before, during, and after your divorce—and keeping the idea of positions vs. interests in mind will help keep your discussions productive.

It's not as hard as you think to focus on interests and not just positions. What may be hard, however, is listening to your spouse when he is saying something you don't want to hear. But you're going to commit to this process and you're going to hear your spouse out—even if you don't get the same in return.

Nobody will ever change his or her mind or position without first feeling that he or she has been heard. So that is where you are going to start. You are going to reframe and rephrase the position. Start with "Let me make sure I understand" and then restate what your spouse has said. Write it down, if you need to. Next, you'll ask for an explanation: "Help me to understand why that is important to you" and "What goal will getting that accomplish for you?" or "What need will that meet?" Say it in a neutral, curious tone. This is about finding out why your spouse wants what she wants and then figuring out a way to give it to her that also feels good to you.

And if it's something that you can't agree to, or figure out how to agree to, at least your spouse knows you listened and considered her wishes. That will go a long way in helping your spouse to compromise, too, when it's about something that's important to you.

Be very clear that you're willing to consider your spouse's position. You don't have to agree on the spot. Ask for time to think about it. But first you need to understand the position and what interests it meets.

If you're not sure you'll agree to the request, you can say, "I am not sure I'll be able to agree to that exact request, but would you be willing to consider a different way to accomplish that goal?" For example, "I'd love to be able to say that I'd waive spousal support. I know how much it irks you to have to pay me. I'd be willing to consider a waiver or shorter time period if we can figure out a way to help me be self-supporting within twelve months. Would you be willing to consider something like that?" Or "I know that you want 50/50 custody, but I am not convinced that the homework will get done when the kids are with you. It was always my job in the marriage since I was the math major. What kinds of safeguards can we build in to make sure the homework gets done? And what will we do if it doesn't get done?"

SWEAT THE SMALL STUFF

Start with the small stuff and work your way up. Don't try to tackle the biggest and hardest problem first. Save that for last. Start with easy things, like your checking accounts and frequent flier miles. Don't start with the house, Christmas parenting time, or valuing your small business. When you start with the big issues, you'll rarely reach an agreement. If you can't solve the small stuff, you won't be able to solve the big stuff. Keep your initial goals small and easy to accomplish.

Working your way up also helps to build trust and confidence in the process. And it lets you see the progress you've made. Even if you can't resolve everything, you can at least narrow down what you still need to tackle. Once you and your spouse see that it's working, your agreement will start to gain momentum. You'll be excited by the prospect that you might actually be able to settle this after all. And the bigger issues might just fall into place.

If you need to generate options, you can begin with what you already know is working, like alternating weekends on your parenting schedule or that one person pays the credit card bills and the other person reimburses for his or her half at the end of the month.

Make sure you know what each person's agreement will need to contain. Again, we're talking goals here, not positions. "I need to be financially secure" or "I want to finish school" or "I want the children to have a close relationship with my parents, even though they live a thousand miles away" are possible elements in your agreement.

THINK CREATIVELY

If you get stuck, consider brainstorming. We love brainstorming because it gets spouses to work cooperatively. Since there's no judgment in brainstorming, you can feel free to throw out ideas for the list. Sure, some will be preposterous. If you start laughing, then great. But the process will also help you to open up your thinking and to think creatively about how to solve these problems. It may be that possible trades will emerge as solutions. Maybe one spouse takes the newer car and the other takes the old truck and also gets the boat. Maybe one parent takes the kids to visit her parents for a month in the summer then the other parent gets them most of winter break.

WHEN YOU ARE TEMPTED TO QUIT

Negotiating your divorce is one party you don't want to stay at too long. Whether it's the entire divorce or just one issue, like dividing up the personal property, rather than rushing things, agree to meet for only a couple of hours, and you'll go as far as you can go in that time. If you can't get it all done in one meeting, then you'll set up another meeting. Don't push it.

Have a time-out agreement. If either of you feels like enough is enough, all you have to do is say so and the other person agrees to agree and stop talking about a particular subject, or to end the meeting. You can always start up again later, but if you get into a fight because you pushed too long, got tired, and then got cranky, you may never come back to the table. Better to postpone a hot issue or meet another time. There's no blue ribbon for getting your divorce settled in one marathon session. You've got time. After all, you didn't get into this situation in two hours, and it's going to take more than two hours to get out of it.

IF THINGS AREN'T GOING AS HOPED

If the negotiations aren't going as smoothly as you'd hoped, ask yourself:

- Are my requests and expectations reasonable given our situation and the law?

- If I were my spouse, would I accept the proposals I'm making?

- Are my offers fair? Would other people perceive them as fair?

- Are my proposals based on facts that I can prove, like the size of our bank account? If so, does my spouse have the information to know that what I'm asking for is accurate?

- Is timing an issue? Am I pushing too hard, too fast, or going more quickly than my spouse can tolerate?

- Is the settlement I'm requesting in line with other court decisions or settlements?

- Do I have the power to force this issue? How likely am I to win if I do force it?

- What are the benefits to me of pursuing my present course? Are there any risks?

Nobody Is Ever Rational

It's tempting to think that if your spouse were just being rational, your divorce would be simple. Never forget that the "interests" described earlier in this chapter are merely a rational, logical, sensible set of concerns, and that people involved in a divorce may have nonrational interests as well. Revenge, reparations for hurt feelings, apologies, shame, guilt, embarrassment, public perceptions . . . the list can be endless. Simply appealing to the logical component often won't be sufficient to complete a settlement or overcome an impasse. It may be that one or both of you are not yet ready to contemplate a true resolution of the conflicts at hand, or it may be that you need to explore these other, nonmonetary benefits.

You won't be able to control your spouse's feelings or behavior, but by using the 8 keys to resolving family conflicts; the 8 peace practices; dealing with your fear, anger, and grief; forgiving yourself and your spouse; and then setting your personal GPS to goodness and walking your talk, you're going to have a huge influence over your interactions with your spouse. It will be very difficult for your spouse to continue to behave poorly when you're walking your talk.

When you set your own goals and are ready to think about different ways of accomplishing them, you begin to open up the range of possibilities for settling your divorce sooner rather than later. By opening up the discussion to your spouse about his or her goals and interests, too, you start on the path to a settlement that not only works for everyone but also lasts.

CHAPTER 11

New Beginnings

Where there's a way, there's a will.

—GARSON KANIN

You've heard "where there's a will, there's a way," but where there's a way, there's also a will. It's hard to muster the courage to do what you know you need to do when you don't know the way to go about it. But now you know how to create a peaceful divorce. You know how to make divorce work.

The skills you've learned, from 8 keys to resolving family conflicts and 8 peace practices, to how to walk your talk and negotiate for what you want and what you need, will keep you on the path toward a peaceful divorce and redefinition of your family. You are, after all, still family. By continuing to use and perfect these skills, you're creating peace in the world, one family at a time.

There will be times when it seems impossible. There will be

people who will try to knock you off of your path. But you can do this. And if you can't do it perfectly, you can do it better than you did it yesterday and better than the day before that.

So what now?

Start by periodically reevaluating your divorce mission statement. How did you do? If you could go back, what would you change?

It's also time to set some new goals. What's your new mission statement for your life after divorce?

New Beginnings Mission Statement

> **We cannot solve our problems with the same thinking that we used when we created them.**
>
> —ALBERT EINSTEIN

Just as you formulated a plan to carry you through a peaceful divorce, you will also need a plan for this new chapter in your life. To create your new beginnings mission statement, start by reading through the following lists and choosing the statements from each that resonate most with your core values. Choose as many as you'd like. You may also determine that there are other things that are important to you that do not appear on these lists. You will use the information you collect about yourself as a starting point to write a mission statement.

1. NOW THAT I AM SINGLE,
   I WANT FOR THE FOLLOWING TO BE TRUE:

- I can take care of myself, and I enjoy taking care of myself.

- My children have two supportive parents committed to co-parenting.

- I am proud of the work I've done toward finishing my degree or advancing my career.

- I've taken the opportunity to reinvent some other parts of my life that were unhappy.

- I still respect my former spouse, and our relationship is friendly, cordial, and civil.

- I have been able to let go of past conflicts, forgive, and move on.

- I realize my marriage was not a complete mistake and value the years I was with my spouse.

- I value what I learned about myself during my divorce and it made me a better person.

- Because of the way I handled my divorce, I'm ready to move on and be a good partner to someone else, or I'll be ready soon.

- I take responsibility for any feelings of abandonment, rejection, fear, anger, grief, and guilt I have, without blaming, shaming, or guilting my spouse or anyone else.

- I do not feel stigmatized by my divorce and refuse to stigmatize others' divorces.

- I'm proud that I handled such a tough situation with so much maturity.

2. I WILL MAKE SURE THAT THE ABOVE ITEMS HAPPEN BY DOING THE FOLLOWING:

- I will ask for advice and support from people who are a positive influence, and then follow that advice.

- I will use the 8 keys to resolving family conflict and the 8 peace practices that I like best when opportunities arise.

- I will take responsibility for my own healing, whether it's financial or emotional.

- I will take emotional care of myself by asking for what I need from people who are able to meet my needs. In turn, I won't take advantage of their graciousness and generosity.

- I will take physical care of myself by getting enough sleep, eating right, maintaining good grooming, and staying safe.

- I will forgive myself and my spouse for getting divorced.

- I will focus on moving forward rather than getting bogged down in the past.

- I will not engage in self-destructive behavior like self-medicating with food, alcohol, drugs, or cigarettes.

- I will seek professional help (clergy, counselor, doctor, etc.) if I feel like I need it.

- I will spend time alone and become reacquainted with myself now that I'm single, and I will not jump right into another relationship.

- I will focus on what is important, both short term and long term, and I'll make sure my actions support my goals.

- I will use written goals to track my progress.

- I will allow myself time to feel fear, anger, and grief as these emotions arise.

- I will focus on positive thoughts like trust and gratitude.

3. FIVE YEARS FROM NOW, I WANT TO FEEL:

- The satisfaction of having been the best person that I could be during this process and afterward

- That I did, and continue to do, the right thing by my children, former spouse, extended family, and friends

- That I met and embraced the challenge of beginning my new single life and that, as a result, I've thrived

- Proud that I am a role model for conflict resolution for my children, family, coworkers, and friends

- Ready to find love again and to trust that I can be intimate and connected with someone else, whether that's in a friendship or a romantic relationship

- Glad that I didn't have to hit rock bottom first before starting to recover from this breakup

- Comfortable with my ex-in-laws ("outlaws") and our mutual friends

- Comfortable attending my children's extracurricular events when my spouse will also be in attendance

- Proud that I not only moved on from past hurts but apologized for and made right any wrongs that I was involved in

- Fully adjusted to my lifestyle and new financial situation

- Proud that I can take care of myself rather than depend solely on my former spouse or anyone else

- Courageous about facing challenges

- Forgiveness and empathy toward myself and my spouse for the hurts we caused each other

- That my divorce, though sad, was a success

- Strong, secure, and satisfied that our settlement was a win-win for all involved

YOUR NEW BEGINNINGS MISSION STATEMENT

Using the items you selected from the checklists or other statements you thought of on your own, pick the three most important from each category and write out your new beginnings mission statement using this formula (feel free to paraphrase):

Now that I am single I am [insert the three items you selected

---

JOE'S NEW BEGINNINGS MISSION STATEMENT

Now that I am single, I am proud of the way I handled my divorce and that I've been able to let go of past conflicts, to forgive, and to move on. I value what I learned about myself during my divorce and it made me a better person. Because of my divorce I'll actually be a better partner than I was in my previous marriage. I'll do this by using the keys to resolving family conflict that I like best, taking responsibility for my own healing, and by taking emotional and physical care of myself and not jumping right into another relationship. I'll set and meet goals and make sure that my actions support my goals. As a result, in five years I will feel like a new person. I will have embraced the challenge of beginning my new single life, and because I'm not still struggling under the weight of a failing relationship, I'll thrive. I'll find new opportunities both socially and at work. I'll be proud that I was a role model for divorce and conflict resolution and grateful that I didn't have to hit rock bottom before starting my new life.

from list 1]. I'll do this by [insert the three items you selected from list 2]. As a result, in five years I will feel [insert the three items you selected from list 3].

Celebrate Your Progress

How did you do with the 8 keys to resolving family conflict? Have you seen the power of listening? Of using "I" statements? What would you like to work on and improve next?

Have you integrated the 8 peace practices into your life? Isn't it amazing how much just remembering to breathe helps you get through a difficult time?

And as for the people in your life, have you learned to set good boundaries with them? Are you able to respond constructively to their unsolicited advice and their opinions? What is your own view of your divorce? Have you been able to let go of some of your negative feelings about divorce in general? Have you been able to forgive yourself and your spouse for getting divorced? By looking at the breakdown of your marriage as a long-term process, a subtle erosion, you can begin to see the contributions that each of you made to the end of your marriage. It's never just one-sided. It's important to be able to have a balanced view of your divorce, and if you're not there yet, you'll get there in time. Learning from this marriage and divorce will improve your relationships in the future.

Think of the people you've met who can't wait to tell you how awful their former spouse is. They don't realize that this reflects on them as much, or more, than it does on their former spouse. After all, who would marry the monster they describe? Only someone with terrible judgment and with no insight or foresight. Who would want to be involved with someone who makes poor choices like that? But of course the complainers don't realize how their spouse bashing reflects on them.

Setting your emotional GPS to goodness gets you most of the way there. When your intention is to do the right thing, most of the time you *will* do the right thing. And when you get off track, you'll realize it sooner than if you hadn't set the intention to stay on the high road. Nobody stays on the high road all the time. But you'll find yourself on the low road less and less when you keep your focus on walking your talk. As you learn to deal more constructively with fear and anger, you begin to take the sting out of these. As you face them head-on, they become much less scary.

When you asked yourself the question "If my best friend told me about the same problem, what would my advice be?" and you realized that you'd reassure that friend and stay optimistic, you may have recognized how hard we are on ourselves. We can be so critical of ourselves, while forgiving of other people. It's time to give ourselves the same benefit of the doubt that we give others.

And when we forgive ourselves, let go of grudges, leave the sins of the past behind, and truly let go, we free ourselves up to remember the positive things in our lives. By practicing the gratitude exercise every day, we cultivate an increasingly optimistic outlook on life. And there is much to be thankful for. It's just easy to miss it when we're having a bad day.

We have so much more control over our divorce and recovery than we think that we do. Let's face it, we're not victims. And if we were victims, we're not victims anymore. We can unilaterally change how people treat us and react to us when we use good boundaries, listening skills, "I" statements, and conflict resolution tools. And as you've seen, you don't have to be a professionally trained mediator to put this into practice. Each little step you make toward peacemaking will change your life. Over time, the impact will be huge.

The positive impact that your new peacemaking skills will have on your life starts small, just like the problems in your marriage started so subtly. And they'll grow over time just like the problems in your marriage did, too. But this will be positive growth. As you use and apply these skills in your redefined family and work life, with friends, and with extended family, you'll see the impact that they have and the profound effect they have on your well-being. When you can say to your critical elderly parent, "Dad, I have a feeling that something is bothering you but that it's not what we're discussing," and it opens the door for him to tell you his worst fears, then you'll know you're there. When you step in to defuse a tense situation between your colleagues at work and encourage them to listen to one another, and you watch them resolve their own problem, you'll know you're there. When you coach a friend to say, "I'm sorry this situation has come to this," to someone with whom he hasn't spoken in two years, and the floodgates of apology and reconciliation open, you'll know you're there.

You can create peace in the world, one family at a time. Keep us posted. Join the interactive community on www.making divorcework.com. As we learn more about forgiveness, negotiation, peace practices, and ways to resolve family conflict, we'll share it with you there. And we can't wait to hear your stories about how you met the challenges, overcame difficulties, and emerged a better person.

RESOURCES

Ben-Zvi, Daniel, "Mediation Worksheet" (2003).

Blackstone-Ford, Jann, PsyD, and Sharyl Jupe, *Ex-Etiquette for Parents: Good Behavior After a Divorce or Separation*. Chicago Review Press, 2004, www.bonusfamilies.com.

Covey, Stephen R., *7 Habits of Highly Effective People: Powerful Lessons in Personal Change*. Deseret Book Company, 2007.

Gottman, John, PhD, *Why Marriages Succeed or Fail*. Simon & Schuster, 1995.

Gottman, John, PhD, *10 Lessons to Transform Your Marriage*. Three Rivers Press, 2007.

Holmes, T. H., and R. H. Rahe (1967), "The Social Readjustment Rating Scale." *Journal of Psychosomatic Research* (2): 213–18.

Luskin, Fred, PhD, *Forgive for Good*. Harper One, 2003.

Moore, Christopher R., *The Mediation Process: Practical Strategies for Resolving Conflict, 3rd Edition*. Jossey-Bass, 2003.

Welch, Suzy, *10-10-10: A Life-Transforming Idea*. Scribner, 2009.

ACKNOWLEDGMENTS

The authors would like to acknowledge our publisher and editor at Perigee, John Duff. His vision for this book served as a beacon while his pen (or in twenty-first-century parlance, his "track changes") kept us on the straight and narrow.

Our thanks also go to our agents at Artists and Artisans, Adam Chromy and Jamie Brenner, who believed in this project before we even believed in it ourselves, to Phalen "Chuck" Hurewitz, without whose insistence this book never would have happened, and Angela Januzzi, our inspired and tireless publicist.

We are grateful to Forrest (Woody) Mosten for teaching us everything worth knowing about how to become a mediator. And our heartfelt thanks go to Nell Merlino and her dedicated staff at Make Mine a Million $ Business (a program that supports innovative businesses with a network of resources, business education, and community support for women wishing to grow micro businesses into million-dollar enterprises), without whom we may have lost the courage to continue our vision of peace in the world, one family at a time.

And perhaps a first for a book's acknowledgments page, we are thankful to Facebook for reuniting the authors after twenty-five years, along with our wildly supportive network friends from North Central High School in Indianapolis.

And finally, we'd like to thank OPEN by American Express (yes, our credit card company!) for trusting us before they should have.

Diana Mercer would also like to thank her father, Victor H. Mercer, DDS, MSD, for teaching her that a true professional not only serves clients but also advances the field. Both are the intention of this book. She thanks her husband, Steve, for his unwavering support and patience, and for making everything worth it every day. She's also grateful to Katie Jane Wennechuk for her inspiration, dedication to this project, and unflappable optimism, as well as her friendship.

Katie Jane Wennechuk would like to thank her mother, Jane Wennechuk, for instilling in her a love of learning through books. She thanks her husband, Robert Lee Thomas, for his ability to love her through all that comes with marriage. She'd also like to thank Diana Mercer for being a true friend and brilliant partner.

INDEX

Abandonment, 90, 233
Abuse, substance, 182
Acceptance, 5, 18, 34, 121, 159, 166, 184, 188, 189
  of divorce, 3, 202
  of failure, 78, 80, 174–75
  of feelings, 166, 185, 187, 197, 234
  of imperfection, 78, 80, 193, 197
  of responsibility, 8, 22–23, 30, 36, 44, 45, 78, 97, 101
Acknowledgment, 40, 43, 60
  of feelings, 42, 95
Acting out, 15
Addiction, 95. *See also specific addictions*
  quitting, 112
Admiration, 12
  mutual, 31
Advice, 155, 237
  asking for, 8, 233
  financial, 215
Affairs, 11, 119–20, 123
Affection, 12, 31, 32
  withholding, 28
Age, 171
Aggression, 59
  passive, 26, 109
Agreements, 100, 211, 227
  creating lasting, 43
Alcohol, 26, 62, 127, 234
  quitting, 112
Alimony, 222
Alone time, 101–2, 112, 234
Alternatives, 115
  increased, 222

Anchoring technique, 54, 57–58
Anger, 5, 8, 18, 24, 26, 29, 46, 51, 60, 61, 76, 89, 90, 103, 108, 114, 165, 166, 175, 233
  dealing with, 102, 128, 176–80, 229, 238
  expressing, 200
  holding on to, 189
  layers of, 58–59, 95
  moving through, 193
  releasing, 180
Anxiety, 113, 116
  reducing, 48
Apologies, 50, 60, 91, 96, 109, 120, 145, 190, 191, 192, 229, 235
Appearance, 172
  fake, 26
  improving, 112
  physical, 156, 234
Appreciation, 92
Arguments, 3, 79, 80, 88
Assertiveness, 103
Assets, value of, 206, 207
Attachment, to things, 119, 129, 134
Attention
  getting, 192
  to process, 81, 118
  selective, 64–65
Attitude, 71, 157, 175, 222
Attraction
  to conflict, 4, 88–89
  weakened, 27, 30
Attractiveness, 12, 172
  physical, 31, 32
Authenticity, commitment to, 107–8

Finances, 2, 4, 5, 11, 12, 31, 33, 114,
115, 119, 139, 217–18
adjusting to new, 235
advice on, 215
fairness of, 7
fear about, 169–70
goals regarding, 125–26, 133
irresponsibility with, 193–94
responsibility with, 169–70
security of, 14, 59, 220
Fitness, 33, 36
Flirting, 33
Focus
on goals, 138–39, 141
on positivity, 136–38, 203
on problems vs. blame, 40–42
Forgiveness, 3, 8, 101, 105, 109, 184,
233, 235, 236
benefits of, 193–202
exercise, 201–2
exercise for self, 198–99
gift of, 189
gratitude and, 203
meaning of, 190–91
practical, 190–91, 199–201, 204
refusing, 192
self, 195–98, 229, 234, 237, 238
of shortcomings, 77
of spouse, 229, 237, 239
Friend(s), 75, 138, 155, 225, 235
confiding in one, 150, 177
losing, 202
relationship with mutual, 72–73,
124–25, 132
sharing, 140
support from, 115, 174, 186
unhelpful, 144
using mutual, 143
Frustration, 14–15, 46, 70
Future, 8
readiness for, 189

Games, playing, 29, 42
Generosity, 202, 224
Goals, 6, 9, 34, 163, 236. *See also*
Divorce mission statement; New
beginnings mission statement

accomplishing, 134, 229–30
areas of setting, 118–34
articulating, 102
behavior and, 50
emotional, 127–28, 133
financial, 125–26, 133
focus on, 138–39, 141
regarding health, 126–27, 133
interest-based, 121–29, 131–34
living according to, 136
progress and, 8
setting personal, 3, 4, 7, 101, 107,
108–13
settlement, 211–24, 220
settlement, exercise, 215–19
settlement, of spouse, 223–24
of spouse, 216, 218–19, 230
written, 234
Goodness, 3
setting emotions for, 76–78,
229, 238
Gossip, 70, 125, 144
Gottman, John, 16
Gratitude, 72, 106, 157, 187,
234, 236
exercise, 203, 238
forgiveness and, 203
Grief, 3, 5, 8, 64, 75, 76, 163, 167, 233.
See also Sadness
allowing, 185
coping with, 128, 229
five stages of, 165–66, 168–88, 189
Grudges, 4, 106
holding, 189, 192, 200, 202, 225
letting go of, 238
Guilt, 2, 8, 14, 17, 27, 34, 35, 36, 40,
70, 76, 97, 107, 108, 145, 146, 154,
197, 229, 233
relief from, 86, 109

Habits, 26
self-destructive, 78
Happiness, 3, 9, 34, 35, 36, 40, 50–51,
77, 82, 86, 104, 128, 157, 182
hopes of, 72
Haters, ignoring, 145, 146
Healing, 8, 36, 75, 95, 107, 234

Linda Russell, Mugshots Photography

Diana Mercer is an attorney-mediator and the founder of Peace Talks Mediation Services in Los Angeles, which operates in a unique multidisciplinary co-mediation model, teaming attorneys with therapists and accountants to resolve divorce, custody, prenuptial, and other family law disputes.

She is a graduate of the Indiana University School of Law, where she received the American Jurisprudence Award for Excellence. She received her undergraduate degree from Indiana University in Economics and French, and she is a member of the Mortar Board Honor Society for Service and Academics. Mercer is an Advanced Practitioner Member of the Association for Conflict Resolution and is admitted to practice law in California, New York, Connecticut, and Pennsylvania and before the Supreme Court of the United States. Mercer, who is widely published in the mediation field, lectures frequently at law schools and professional conferences on both mediation and career development. She is the cochair of the American Bar Association Dispute Resolution Services Practice Development Committee and is known nationwide for her expertise in marketing alternative dispute resolution services.

Mercer is the coauthor of *Your Divorce Advisor: A Lawyer and a Psychologist Guide You Through the Legal and Emotional Landscape of Divorce* with Marsha Kline Pruett, PhD, MSL.

Paul Nichols

Katie Jane Wennechuk is a certified divorce mediator and chief communications officer for Peace Talks Mediation Services in Los Angeles. Wennechuk received a bachelor's degree in English from Indiana University and a master's degree in communications from Western Michigan University. She has professional training in diplomacy and negotiation. For many years she worked with leading authors and publishers in the human potential and New Age areas, including Marianne Williamson and Namaste Publishing.

Visit the authors' website at www.makingdivorcework.com.

PEACE TALKS

Peace Talks Mediation Services' team of attorneys and therapists offers a constructive, forward thinking and peaceful ending to relationships.

Marriages may end, but families endure.

Our services include all aspects of family law mediation: divorce, custody, child support, parenting plans, financial settlements, and premarital agreements.

Peace Talks' goal is to take everything that people hate about the family law system and do the opposite. Our mission is to create peace in the world one family at a time.

For more information, resources, and divorce-planning tools, visit us at www.peace-talks.com.

And to find a Peace Talks Mediation Services office near you, give us a call at (310) 301-2100.